AF522375

EVEN THE PAST SPEAKS

Fragments of Ancient Indian History and Culture

Prof. S.N. Agnihotri

EVEN THE PAST SPEAKS

Fragments of Ancient Indian History and Culture

Essays in Tribute to Prof. S.N. Agnihotri

Edited by
Anup Kumar

"Lives of great men
All remind us
We can make
Our lives sublime."

H.W. Longfellow

There is only one man in this world who has selflessly woven the thread of his love into the fabric of our life. You are not only a modern shrawan kumar but a loving husband as well as super dadda and apart from that a beautiful soul who has turned up best in all the relations. While going through the lane of dreams, you will always be there to carry us in your arms during every unfortunate situation and your blessings will protect us from every possible serious repercussions and this is the blind trust on our superman papa. We miss you a lot.

With Love
Your Family

First Published, 2016

ISBN 978-93-83723-15-7

Published by
LG PUBLISHERS DISTRIBUTORS
49, Gali No. 14, Pratap Nagar
Mayur Vihar Phase I, Delhi 110 091
Tel : 011 2279 5641 email: lgpdist@gmail.com

Printed at
Sapra Brothers, Delhi 110 092

To my wife

Anita

Contents

Preface

In the year 2006, I got an opportunity to work in a small but dynamic part of Gandhi Faiz-e-Aam College, Shahjahanpur. The martyrdom of Ramprasad Bismil, Ashfaq Ullah Khan, Roshan Singh popularized the city called *The City of Martyrs*. Moreover, in the north end of the city was the famous Dunde Khan Bagh which, in history, is popular as a place where the battle of 1857 against the British was fought. In 1947, during the time of Indian partition, when the whole country was under social and political upheaval, bloodshed and anarchy prevailed all around, people were migrating and in all these adverse situations Janab Fazl-Ur-Rahman Khan was laying the foundation stone of Gandhi Faiz-e-Aam College based on the principles of Gandhiji, in the same bagh.

When I departed from the Ganga-Jamuna culture of Allahabad and reached Shajahanpur, a city situated between Garra and Khannaut rivers, it did not seem to me less charming than Allahabad. The city is well known for its communal harmony, secularism, patriotism and human identity. The sacrificial nature and simplicity of the citizens attracted me towards them.

Undoubtedly, no one in the world is perfect but, of course, the qualities of one's personality make a person different from the others. Prof. Srawan Nath Agnihotri (Panditji) was a unique personality. Hard work, entrepreneurship, spirituality and dedication were his characteristics. But his selfless dedication and devotion for the mother institute became a major source of inspiration for me. We worked together for nine years. Though a scholar of physics, I found him very keen on the social sciences. History, philosophy, literature, theology were his favourite subjects and were the centre of all our discussions. His motivational spirit and dynamic personality helped me in the difficult tasks of academic programmes and creative writing.

Prof. Agnihotri in cooperation with Prof. Uday Prakash Arora successfully organized the Indian History Congress in 2004 at MJP Rohilkhand University, Bareilly. In 2010, I organized the UP History Congress at Gandhi Faiz-e-Aam College with his help. Moreover, history had become his favourite subject. Prof. Om Prakash, Prof. Uday Prakash Arora, Prof. Mushirul Hasan, Prof. K.C. Yadav, Prof. Atul Kumar Sinha, such great historians were very dear to him. So I feel privileged to associate the book entitled *Even the Past Speaks* with him. The book is in two parts; the first part is the expression of the feelings and tributes to the great soul Prof. Agnihotri and the second part comprises essays by historians.

Prof. Agnihotri was born in June 1947 in an ordinary Brahmin family of Sahjahanpur. He did his high school in 1959, intermediate in 1963 and B.Sc. from Gandhi Faiz-e-Aam College Shahjahanpur in 1963. In 1965, Allahabad University awarded him an M.Sc. in Physics. The same year, he was appointed as lecturer in the department of physics at Gandhi Faiz-e-Aam College Shahjahanpur. His dedication to the mother institute and his devotion to Gandhian principle had made him the first non-minority Principal of the college in 2004 and in 2007, after his retirement he even more enthusiastically started serving the institute without any salary. He was so enthusiastic to his duty that he used to say, *'If I do not see the mirror I feel like a youngman of eighteen years.'* He died on January 7, 2014.

He worked regularly for the development of the institute. He started new professional and traditional courses in the college under the self-finance scheme. As a keen scholar he was looking for a centre for academic activities. His optimistic vision and dynamic personality always proved the phrase, "Where there is a will there is a way" and consequently he established Fazl-Ur-Rahman Khan Advanced Research Centre for the quality research in social sciences and humanities. Haji Jamiluddin Khan Central Library of the centre is one of the few libraries of the country. Moreover, the advanced research centre aims to explore the value-based research in history, culture, art, tradition, philosophy, literature, education, sociology, etc. The main objective of the centre, Prof. Agnihotri used to emphasize, is to expose the futility of the materialistic life and to advocate and promote the value of ethics, traditions and simplicity of life. Modern research, he considered, should inculcate the values and ethics in the new generation. The publication of the *Journal of Social Sciences and Humanities* in 2007 became a very positive step in the same direction.

I am indebted to all the contributors who directly or indirectly helped me in this book dedicated to my mentor the late Prof. Agnihotri. I thank Prof. Zill-ur-Rahman Khan, Prof. U.P. Arora, Prof. H.K. Sharma, Prof. P.R.R. Nayar, Janab Syed Moinuddin, President, Managing Committee, Gandhi Faiz-e-Aam College, Shahjahanpur and Janab Sohail Ashfaq Khan. My thanks are also due to Prof. N. Mudgal whose cooperation and scholarly suggestions helped to form the book into the existing shape. The publisher Mr. Rahul Saxena showed his keen interest in the publication of this book and thanks are due to his help and cooperation. Once again, I thank you all for your support and cooperation.

Anup Kumar

Part I

MEMOIRS AND TRIBUTES

1

Never Seen Such a Person Before

Zill-Ur-Rahman Khan

Only in the last few years of S.N. Agnihotri's life, I came to know that he was a lecturer in Physics at G.F. College. He served there for about 40 years, in all. After seven-eight years of service, he began helping the college in going to different places on its behalf. For all this time, he was doing things in which he had no say at all. This continued for several decades. I hear that during all this time, he was regarded as a good teacher.

He served under four presidents, two from my family, including my father and two of Haji Jameel Uddin Khan Sahib's. family, including Haji Sahib himself. He was a faithful follower of Haji Sahib. He followed what Haji Sahib told him or later, what his nephews told him. He followed what he was told and tried to do his best.

He was an able person, polite to people and tried to help people, if possible.

He never wanted to harm anybody. Hard work and facing adversity with a smile were his hallmarks. He ate and lived simply.

In the early days, he knew many Hindutava top people. In his later days, he came to know people like Syed Noorul Hasan Sahib and Jyoti Basu. Both of them impressed him.

He came into contact with many Muslims in Shahjahanpur. Then he met people from different states, different walks of life, etc. That balanced his outlook very much. Gandhi and Nehru had a strong influence on him. He also read extensively about Dr. Zakir Husain.

In this way, he came to know of Muslims in the freedom movement. All these influences made him a moderate.

At the time of the destruction of the Babri Masjid he was in Calcutta and near Jyoti Basu. Agnihotri told us that the reaction of the demolition on Jyoti Basu was very strong. An ordinary person would not have understood it. It was the reaction of a most highly cultured, refined and humanist Hindu. He saw the Hindu in him for the first time. The Marxist in him would also have been present, but he was saying something like India had nothing of a past left. Here was the best of Jyoti Basu.

When the election results appeared on TV, after Indira Gandhi was killed, a journalist asked Jyoti Basu, in Agnihotri's presence, the cause of the Marxist defeat, Jyoti Basu said, 'We have served the people a great lot, but not given our life for the country like that'.

Haji Jameel Uddin Khan Sahib embarked on an ambitious programme of development in the college about 15 years ago. Many labs, buildings and an additional library were built. These were positive developments. Quite a few of these bore my father's name. That was one reason for my softness towards the college during the last three-four years, one should not go on opposing something just for the sake of opposing it. So, I changed my views and said I would support positive programmes of the college administration.

Agnihotri told me particularly that he was a staunch supporter of the minority character and for maintaining the social composition of the three colleges under the management.

Two-three years ago, I tactfully mentioned that a little more effort was required to have more Muslim teachers in the Self-Finance Programme. So, for this purpose, Agnihotri and I went to Aligarh and Delhi on this programme, and met many people, but not a single Muslim came that year.

On the whole, the development programme ran fairly well for several years, but in the last couple of years, the programme seemed to be getting out of hand and I pointed out once towards the social composition getting upset. Agnihotri agreed but expressed helplessness but hoped that it might be temporary.

Near the end, once I went with him to Lucknow and saw that the end was near. There, he went to meet some officers and came out in two minutes. The same happened at another place. Then, I knew his best efforts were failing. I knew the college had made a great effort and could not do more. The help was not coming to it from where it was expected.

I heard the same scene had been enacted on his last visit to Lucknow. He travelled more than anyone could. He used to come at 4 a.m. and leave at 4 p.m. This happened till the last day of his life.

It was no one's fault. The programme was too demanding and ambitious. Everyone tried to do his best. There is no doubt about that. The college authorities cooperated with him fully from the beginning to the end. Problems arose, but, fortunately, they seem to have been solved by now. I am sure any remaining problems would now be more easily solved. One must say the authorities always did their best.

A great effort was made. Let us hope it has temporarily failed. New people will come and take it to a grand finale. Now, there should be no blame game. Let us remember Agnihotri as the first servant he loved to call himself.

Let there be a grand reconciliation.

My best wishes to all.

2

In Remembrance of a Lovable Departed Soul—Prof. S.N. Agnihotri

Om Prakash

Though a postgraduate of my own Alma Mater, University of Allahabad, I knew Prof. Agnihotri more intimately after joining the office of Vice-Chancellor of MJP Rohilkhand University, Bareilly. The Gandhi Faiz-e-Aam College, Shahjahanpur is one of the best colleges of the University enjoying the most exceptional distinction of being founded during the partition of the country and its bloody aftermath proclaiming in its name the two national figures symbolizing Hindu-Muslim unity in India in the land of freedom movement revolutionary Ram Prasad Bismil. The College thus has a monumental value and significantly Prof. Agnihotri was its first Hindu Principal. Unconcerned about his personal looks and even unmindful of whether he had his morning shave or not, when he met me, I always saw him in more or less the same winter or summer attire holding a water bottle to his chest. He was already the Principal of the College for one year when he first met me and retired from his post when I was in the middle of my term in 2007. The chemistry between him and the President (Haji Jamiluddin Khan Sahib) and the management of the minority College was so strong that immediately after his retirement he was made incharge of all the self-financing courses run by the College. The trust of the President in him deepened much more after his retirement. Haji Sahib was such a noble soul that he could annoy anybody but the Panditji, as he called Agnihotriji his friend and favourite since his school days informally in love. He cared for him less like a brother but more like a mother, caring for the minutest of his comforts and conveniences which were not even mentioned by the latter.

As I knew him, Agnihotriji had totally dedicated himself to the College, its students and teachers. He lived more in the College than in his own house. His family very often missed him and had to enquire about his whereabouts for the saintly President of the College. Student and teacher of physics, Agnihotriji strived for humanities as a missionary. Needless to say, this mission of his had the blessings of his President who had inherited nationalism from the founder of the College Fazl-ur-Rahman Khan Sahib a close relative of another known nationalist who rose to be India's President Dr. Zakir Husain. A great educationist, he founded the Jamia Millia Islamia in Delhi. For a College of this background, nationalism and humanities always went together, science, physics and technology notwithstanding. Time and again the Panditji was deputed to invite me for a lecture to the audience which included the faculty, students, members of the management and distinguished guests from the town on sundry topics such as history, education and political movements touching on the present. Such fervour for interactional academic sessions has been a rarity then and even now. Nobody is ready to recognize the regenerative value of such sessions in generating a research temper side by side with deep humanitarian concerns so much lacking even in the biggest academic institutions of the country. That was why I never refused his requests, if I had time.

The Management of the College sprang a surprise in the line of this basic approach lying deep in its inception when it instituted an Award of Rs. one lakh and decided to confer it firstly on the Human Resource Development Minister, Shri Arjun Singh at a simple function held in the Campus of Jamia Millia Islamia, Delhi. At about the same time, the College decided to found the Fazl-ur-Rahman Khan Advanced Research Centre for quality research in Social Sciences and Humanities. Its Library was named after the President of the College the late Haji Jamiluddin Khan Sahib after his sad demise. The moving spirit of all these institutional expansions was undoubtedly Prof. S.N. Agnihotri. That is why he has been running from place to place day and night to facilitate and negotiate many things on behalf of the College. His retirement from the job of the Principal could never come in his way due to the nationalist and humanitarian temper of the Presidents and Management of the College past and present. The Panditji had the knack to inspire teachers and students of the College to work overtime with him in giving his dream project a concrete shape. He also strived hard for bringing in Research Fellowships and projects for the Centre and visited practically every book fair in Delhi with a view to enriching its Library so long as he lived. His dream was to make the Centre a hub of Sanskrit, Persian, epigraphic, numismatic and archaeological studies and advanced research. To propagate the vast mission of the Centre he also launched the journal entitled *The Journal of Social Sciences and Humanities* and a magazine *Charkha*. On his initiative the College hosted a session of the UP History Congress in its campus.

Agnihotriji was a man of great ideas, nationalist zeal and a dashing executor of great ideas and decisions very often initiated by him and others. He was a noble soul always bearing his sagacity and convictions so lightly in the appearance of a simple man. All of us sustained an irreparable loss in his passing away at a relatively young age. He will always be remembered as a shining star in the world of institutionalizing education on boldly and brilliantly conceived nationalist and secular lines.

3

Prof. S.N. Agnihotri: A Man of Profound Attributes

P.R.R. Nair

I had known Prof. S.N. Agnihotri for over a decade. I came into contact with him when I was Coordinator of the National Commission for Minority Education, of the Ministry of HRD. I was functioning as Registrar of the National University of Educational Planning and Administration (NUEPA) at the relevant time. The commission used to visit various States and Union Territories to interact with state governments, minority educational institutions, other stakeholders, etc. It was during one of these visits to Lucknow, where I had spent four years of my life, that I met Prof. Agnihotri, in the Chamber of Shri Rajeev Kumar, the State Education Secretary. We interacted and that was the beginning of a wonderful friendship which blossomed into a lasting relationship. I was impressed by his passion, devotion to duty and diligent nature. He was very concerned about the college and commencement of various academic programmes there. In my own humble way, I could help him in connecting with people and departments at the government level. He always used to make it a point to visit me while in Delhi. I have warm memories of my interaction and friendship with Prof. Agnihotri. His sudden departure has been a personal loss for me.

4

Prof. S.N. Agnihotri: My Friend, Philosopher and Guide

H.K. Sharma

It is giving me immense pleasure to write a few words about my teacher respected, Professor and Principal S.N. Agnihotri. I was his student from July 1970 to June 1972, when I was studying in the intermediate in G.F. College, Shahjahanpur. Prof. Agnihotri was one of the youngest professors of the Physics Department at that time. Although the youngest in age but no doubt the tallest in teaching and career building of the students. It will not be an exaggeration to say that the students of Shahjahanpur who had successfully cleared the PMT from 1968 to 1985 were directly or indirectly under the guidance and supervision of Prof. Agnihotri. His teaching talents had scaled Mount Everest.

Gandhi Faiz-e-Aam College is an embodiment of secularism not in theory but also in practice and I do not have any hesitation in saying that Principal Agnihotri was a true representative of this secularism and great institution. Prof. Agnihotri was closely associated with Prof. Rajendra Singh, popularly known as "Rajju Bhaiyya" who was a Professor of Physics at Allahabad University and Prof. Agnihotri was a student of M.Sc. at that time. But still Prof. Agnihotri's secular credentials were never in doubt. After his retirement as principal he was still very closely associated with the management body of the college and he was virtually instrumental in all developmental projects and opening of new courses in the college. When he died in January 2014 in Lucknow, he was on an official tour related to college work. Perhaps Prof. Agnihotri was born for the students and college and he also died for the same cause.

Whatever, I am today, I frankly admit, that this is because of the fact that a learned, committed, sincere scholar like Prof. S.N. Agnihotri was my friend, philosopher and guide.

Although, Prof. Agnihotri is no more but his principles, noble deeds, and motivation will contine to inspire teachers and taught for an indefinite period.

5

Panditji: A Man of 'Junoon'

U.P. Arora

Panditji was introduced to me for the first time at the fresher's function of Sir Ganganath Jha Hostel of Allahabad University, sometime in August 1962. Although he was one year senior to me in the University, he was junior in the hostel. In the hostel, I always found him engaged in his studies. He was doing his M.Sc. in Physics. The Physics Department of Allahabad University was well-known in the country at that time. Once the luminary like Professor Meghnath Saha headed that Department. Only very brilliant students like Panditji could get admission there.

After leaving Allahabad University as a student, Panditji lost contact with me. I continued to remain as a teacher in Allahabad for nearly two decades. In 1985 when I joined Rohilkhand University I found my lost friend teaching in the reputed Gandhi Faiz-e-Aam College in Shahjahanpur, which is his hometown.

If I have to characterize Panditji in one word it will be 'junooni'. There are many types of junoonis. Some are engaged in a specific game, others in singing or dancing, etc. But the 'junoon' of Panditji was a rare type. I have never come across such an example. His 'junoon' was Gandhi Faiz-e-Aam College and nothing else. He was fully dedicated to his institution. As long as he lived, he lived for the College. The teachers, students and all the non-teaching staff of the College had a great respect for Panditji. Was he a patron of this College? President....? Manager or Principal? He did not hold any administrative post in the College. He was just a teacher. But he was everything for this institution. Whether there was a problem with the UGC, some work with the State Government, University or some other institution, everywhere the crisis was averted only by Panditji. In fact he was in need everywhere in the College. On account of his engagements in the College, he was unable to spare time for his family. His colleagues have informed me that when he had extra work he used to sleep in the College itself. I have never come across a person like him, so dedicated to his institution.

He had one dream. He was interested in developing a research institution in which a solution for various social problems could be worked out by the researchers. The infrastructure which is required for such an institute was nearly completed by him. A big library and building are already in existence for the institute. But unfortunately no progress has been made after his death.

Panditji used to discuss with me the firm organization of that institute. The real homage to Panditji for his fans will be to complete the task left by him. His dreams should be fulfilled.

Part II
ESSAYS

6

Tolerance in Indian Culture

Om Prakash and Anup Kumar

Indian society and culture are supposed to be examples par excellence of peaceful coexistence of innumerable communities, tribes, foreign invaders, nationalities, linguistic, religious, racial and cultural identities over the ages. The history of the subcontinent is also sometimes recounted as a glorious triumph of peaceful assimilation of a number of these components across time. It is in this land alone that subhuman treatment was meted out to untouchables which has been and is still tolerated as a blessing and the masses of common men and women cheerfully tolerated the robbing of their right to education, fruits of their labour and even two square meals a day. Poverty and illiteracy are not better tolerated anywhere else notwithstanding immense accumulation of wealth, luxuries and educational excellence by a privileged few. Wholesale, massacres, treachery and slavery imposed by force by the invaders and foreign rulers too have been tolerated as also the subversion of education and public morality, particularly in matters of handling funds, in independent India. What has not been tolerated in this extremely tolerant society were attempts at mass-conversion by proselytizing alien religions, agitations for human rights and social justice by age-old victims of social discrimination. Established orders of dominance always like to perpetuate inbuilt structural inequalities of our traditional social order as convenient props to their power and position monopolies at any and every cost. Tolerance in reality is, therefore, also far from the general perception of its being a noble virtue or something of extraordinary price. But is it then the equivalent of a mute submission to despotic forces, dishonestly projected as a virtue? Were Asokan proclamations of *ahimsa* and *samavaya* or messages of forbearance and forgiveness of our saints and scriptures hypocrisy, pure and simple? These conflicting perceptions, of tolerance in our culture and society call for history to clear up the notional and factual confusion involved in this matter. Let us begin by analysing our views on Indian culture and society followed by a consolidation of scholarly perceptions about tolerance and finally discussing the concept of tolerance in its multidimensional aspects as a Western and Indian value.

Recognizing Indian culture and the concept and role of tolerance in it poses a multidimensional problem which ought to be analysed first before attempting any formulation of their diagnostic traits. Already a highly complex subjective proposition embodying Western notions of *Vernunft* (Reason), *Bildung* (Education) and *Freitheit* (Freedom), *Kultur* from which the English word culture is derived, assumes an added complexity when its theoretical lopsidedness is corrected by introducing the objectivity of nature united with the aforesaid subjectivity into it through the bond of dialectics introduced by Kierkegaard and Marx.[1] As a sociological concept, culture is again to be distinguished from its spiritual meaning which is its underlying value-system, symbolically apprehended. Referred to India, it becomes all the more intricate in so far as these Western concepts and symbols are stretched beyond their millieu to denote an alien phenomenon. Reflected once through the symbols of its native languages, institutions and art, the pluralistic image of Indian culture is caused to reappear on the mirror of Western concepts and symbols in order to be communicable. In the process are bound to be created optical illusions and distortions from which the subject of our inquiry necessarily suffers. In sum, one of the dimensions of the problems is basically that of communication: the question of expressing the phenomena of a totally different milieu with the symbols and expressions crystallized in an altogether different context.

It is further to be inquired into if our problem is a problem of fact or value. Do we recognize Indian culture as a fact of history and, in order to perpetuate it, our current experience is to be continued in future, or do we look upon it as a scheme of value informing and inspiring our conduct? Writing about Hinduism, M.N. Srinivas and A.M. Shah complain of excessive bibliocentralism of earlier scholars who endeavoured to derive every bit of Indian culture from texts, ignoring the actual institutions, rites and beliefs altogether.[2] As an instance he cites caste which appears to embody the social reality of Indian culture only after the census reports had brought out its factual details in full. Theorizing from this factual data, Dumont has explained the origin of caste through the given of hierarchy conceptualized as the religious distinctions of purity and pollution, not caring that these data represented the end product of India's social experience through the ages.[3] Factual details are no doubt important, but it is probably wrong to call the problem of identifying Indian culture as merely a problem of fact. A non-evaluational generalization from the inductively assembled facts and observation is bound to lead to errors such as those committed by Dumont.[4] Our problem is, therefore, necessarily a problem of value. But generalizing on the basis of normative prescriptions alone without a factual verification, may lead to the assumption that the actual practice never deviated from the rules. In fact, a correct historical appraisal of Indian culture will need both the ideals and facts of life. The attempt of inferring from the present the factual aspects of the past is as dangerous as deriving facts of life from ideals and norms.

Ideals and values are undoubtedly studied in a branch of philosophy known as axiology, but probably philosophy alone will not be able to solve this problem. It can tell us about the nature of values which Indian culture stands for, it can work out logical relations among them, on the one hand, and with the metaphysically conceived universe, on the other. It may also relate different orders of value with the *summum bonum,* besides expounding the need and mode of their seeking. But philosophy will be doing all this without taking into account the gap between theory and practice and the element of change on these two levels. A structural analysis of values is no doubt welcome, but unless they are seen also in their dynamic and diachronic aspects, however slow may be the frequency of change in their case, their account will be necessarily incomplete. If once we realize that the values are not static and permanent, the question of relation of their change with the change on an actual plane and an explanation of the same arises.[5] That is to say, there is history also of philosophy and it ought to be coordinated with the history of life on the factual plane.[6]

This lands us in the domain of historical inquiry—a perspective which this chapter seeks to present. But the job of history too is not free from difficulties. There are so many mutually exclusive and often overlapping focuses of historical inquiry. History unfortunately has its own philosophies, science and theories. If its theories and philosophies are value-laden, its science talks either of value-neutrality or of discovering permanent laws of historical change which are again pursuing a value we call scientificity. As these philosophies, theories and science of history have been formulated in the West in modern times, the values carried by them are necessarily modern and Western. Historical exercise thus runs the risk of substituting from the back door modern Western values as touchstones for those we are going to study in the context of Indian culture.[7] Under this scheme of study modern Western culture is likely to become the measure of all cultures, as the criterion of our final evaluation is bound to be anyone of our value-laden historical theories. For example, if we are trying to understand Indian culture through the Marxist theory of history, can we escape the dichotomy of classes leading to class conflict for the ultimate goal of ending the exploitation of poor by the rich? All the values belonging to Indian culture stand subordinated to this supreme value Marxist historiography, simply because we are using it as a tool. Similarly, if an idealist theory is applied, it will put out of focus the material and nearer-to-earth pursuits of man and the values relating to them, besides introducing stealthily the values of the tool of analysis as the cherished values of Indian culture or as a measure of them. Besides these, there are many more historical modes of looking at Indian culture with a number of dichotomies in view: as for instance, the barbarism and civilization dichotomy which characterized the approach of early missionaries and historians like Archer and others.[8] Then the imperialism and nationalism dichotomy with an explicit attempt on the part of the Imperialist historians to reduce Indian culture to a place of relative inferiority and on the part of nationalist historians to glorify themselves in an historical account of their culture in the past and approaching or excelling the image of their masters in the present.[9] Besides these, there are idealism and materialism, freedom and determinism, individualism and socialism, hierarchical and egalitarian, model-based and model-free dichotomies to which a historical evaluation of Indian culture and its essentials is often subjected. It is necessary to steer clear of these difficulties if we want to keep the object of our inquiry free from these difficulties without mixing it up with other unnecessary issues.

Prevalent Views on Tolerance

Tolerance has been proclaimed as the hallmark of Indian culture, and the sense of synthesis, universal outlook and respect for individuals peculiar to it have been shown as flowing from this central point. The basis of tolerance is supposed to be the overall philosophical outlook characteristic of Indian culture and yet Indian culture is supposed to be neither otherwordly nor asocial, neither fatalistic not wanting in ethical content.[10] Tolerance is sometimes equated with the essence of *dharma* or *Rit* which is the same as the harmony of Cosmic Order, from which creation emerges. To live in conformity with this Cosmic Order and to dedicate oneself to it are supposed to constitute the Highest Good and, in the attempt to realize this, are said to originate virtues like *ahimsa, aparigraha* and *vairagya*—the three forms of tolerance in the sphere of the individual's conduct and a non-competitive hierarchical society idealized as a triumph of discipline, duty and selflessness over egotism, acquisitiveness and hedonism. Fourfold division of hierarchical society is justified on the basis of a factual observation that all men are not equal in their capabilities and aptitudes.[11]

Viewing it in the limited context of Hinduism, W.F. Adeney appears to present the other side of the picture when he says, "It has been asserted that Hinduism is the most tolerant of all religions. This may be true as regards other than Hinduism because, being entirely racial and hereditary, it cannot proselytize.... Hinduism has no opening for such (proselytes). Accordingly it must tolerate alien faiths, unless, like Tibetan Buddhism, it forbids immigration." Generalizing from this, he interprets tolerance as "refraining from prohibition and persecution".[12] It is always according to him, an element of "latent disapproval" granting freedom which is "limited and conditional." It is thus not the same as "religious liberty" or "religious equality", in sum, a thoroughly negative proposition.[13] If we drop the strictly limited context of religion from this definition of tolerance in view of its fairly wide scope in Indian culture, as noted above, the question automatically arises if tolerances in Indian culture is equivalent to liberty and equality. Has it been originally conceived positively or negatively? Is it a virtue of necessity? At least in respect of the ideal of virtuous conquests without annexation, Basham thinks that it was a virtue of necessity.[14] In utter contradiction of what W.F. Adeney says about the Hindu concept of toleration Max Weber thinks, "It is an undoubted fact that, in India, religious and philosophical thinkers were able to enjoy perfect freedom for a long period. The freedom of thought in ancient India was so considerable as to find no parallel in the West before the most recent age."[15] Elucidating the concept of secularism, M.C. Setalvad links this essentially Western concept with the "freedom of religion or religious tolerance in the East" and writes, "Freedom of religion of the individual, which is one of the basic ideas of a secular state, has for centuries, been rooted in Asian countries following the Hindu or Buddhist religion."[16] If tolerance in Hinduism is not the same as religious liberty to some, it is freedom of conscience to others. It it is a virtue of necessity to some, it is the precursor of secularism to others. Why is there such an anarchy of views regarding tolerance in Indian culture?

As a sum of material, acquisitive, social, religious and artistic achievements of different groups unified by common values and beliefs, Indian culture combines the rigidity and social discrimination of castes in its social and material aspects of life with the freedom of conscience or tolerance in the field of religious life. What is the relation between the two? K.M. Munshi and S. Radhakrishnan appear to look upon the hierarchical social order of which the caste system is an extreme expression as an essential corollary of the value of religious tolerance.[17] As this value could not be fulfilled in a competitive, acqusitive and egotistic society, a non-competitive, duty-bound and distinction-ridden society was created as a matter of ideal.[18] But K.M. Panikkar looks upon caste as a "dead tissue"[19] and Setalvad calls it an "incubus" which, still dominating "all aspects of a citizen's activity", has firmly entered politics and plays a powerful role in the selection and election of candidates to the legislative bodies, in the selection of Ministers and in appointments to various public offices." Far from being an essential corollary of the value of tolerance, the thrust of such a social order, according to him, is patently anti-secular and anti-tolerance.[20] Incidentally, it is also to be thought over why a religiously intolerant West could insist on the value of an egalitarian, acquisitive and competetive social order and a religiously tolerant Indian culture developed a rigid, caste-ridden hierarchical social order as a value or disvalue?

Otherworldliness is, at times, suggested as an essential

concomitant of tolerance in Indian culture in as much as it helps to understand all religions as different paths to the same ultimate end. In the social sphere too, it enables the individual to rise above social constraints by taking to *sanyasa,* or renunciation. Basham, however, refutes otherworldliness as an essential trait of Indian culture.[21]

In a sociological characterization of Indian culture, Yogendra Singh has attributed to it the values of hierarchy, holism, continuity and transcendence from his elucidation of these values, it is not clear in which of these the value of tolerance will be included. However, he is of the definite opinion that "of these the hierarchy value constituted the core of value system."[22] As he thinks, "the principle of transcendence represents the values of freedom and human initiative in Indian culture."[23] One may hopefully locate tolerance in this of the four so-called cardinal values of Indian culture. It explains the phenomenon of renunciation quite well, but it hardly does justice to the value of tolerance. As admitted by Singh, his scheme is essentially heuristic, to which one may like to add: and developed as a logical antithesis of the Western values of equality, individualism, historicity and techno-scientific rationalism in order to produce the effect of a complete contract.

The foregoing critical survey of some of the views regarding Indian culture, with special reference to the concept of tolerance in it very clearly shows the state of confusion prevailing on the point. None of these views appears to emerge from within the original sources in which Indian culture is rooted. On the contrary, they appear to be as notions originating in the specific situations of observation and thought and imposed from above as an essential trait of Indian culture. Their heuristic character is unmistakable.

Tolerance as a Religious Concept

Tolerance in Indian culture has been interpreted as a concept narrower than that of religious liberty because its traditional religion, Hinduism, does not proselytize which means that a religion which does not proselytize cannot afford to be intolerant.[24] But we have in history examples of persecution even by adherents of religions which did not proselytize. To give only one example. The Romans are known to have been followers of a traditional religion which did not proselytize and yet they persecuted Christianity. Tolerance was known to Rome but only as an item of the State's policy, and not as an ethos of its culture which was aggressive expansionism.[25] She could not afford to impose her religion on the areas conquered by her and hence she had to be tolerant to the religions of the conquered but she had to be intolerant to Christianity which invaded her own domain religiously.[26] Roman religion could retain its separate existence only so long as the state was persecuting Christianity, but it was devoured by the latter soon after the persecutions were stopped and the patronage withdrawn. Once patronized by the Roman emperors, Christianity itself became a persecuting religion besides being a proselytizing one.[27] Indian traditional religion on the contrary, did not make the traditional state to wage bloody wars against aggressive religions like Buddhism, Jainism, Islam and Christianity, even though the proselytizing activities of Islam were accompanied with the extensive persecution of Hindus by many Muslim rulers.[28] Not only that, it endured the rule of the active and persecuting patrons of some of these alien religions, sometimes for centuries together, without enjoying the support of any political power and yet it saved itself from being wholly absorbed by any of them. This quality of persistence even without the patronage of a political power is a sign of strength, not weakness which all the non-proselytizing, tribal, primitive or polytheistic religions of the world lacked separated from state patronage none of them could survive the persecuting and proselytizing onslaughts and hence traditional Indian religion does not appear to be only one of them. Its unparalleled quality of tolerance is not, therefore, a product of its weakness but an expression of its strength. It did not proselytize because it was sure of its intrinsic strength and the same confidence again prevented it from being fanatical and intolerant.

The policy of religious tolerance in Europe was a precursor of religious liberty, and hence it is in the fitness of things in that context to assign the former a more restricted scope than the latter.[29] The concept of religious liberty owed much to the theory of Natural Law and the process of emergence of the secular state from within the overall religious control of the Christian Church.[30] Much of the bloodshed in religious wars and persecution under the inquisition in Europe was due to the power-game of the Roman Catholic Church rather than to the basically intolerant character of the original Christian doctrine,[31] though more radical thinkers like Rousseau attributed such a character to it and wished to abolish the dogma as such.[32] As Hinduism had neither a church nor a tradition of intolerance associated with its very inception, there was no question of its tolerance being short of a full-fledged religious freedom. Weber is right when he says that Hindu *dharma* is not a religion in the European sense of the term. The meaning of religion is probably exhausted in the Indian concept of *sampradaya* or *mata* which constitutes one of the many paths to the ultimate end of human life as conceived in Hindu *dharma*.[33] If all the roads lead to the same destination there can be no quarrel about the choice of the one or the other of them.[34] This is tolerance within Hinduism and also at the same time a device to synthesize all other non-proselytizing religions and sects to the corpus of Hindu beliefs. The attitude towards the alien proselytizing religions such as Islam and Christianity too was not intolerant, and this tolerance, as shown above, emerged from the will and strength to hold its own against all possible odds.

Tolerance in India is often regarded as the forerunner of the modern concept of secularism enshrined in our constitution as one of the basic characters of our Union. The creed of secularism, as shown by Setalvad, "denotes a way of life and conduct guided by materialist considerations devoid of religion. The basis of the ideology is that material means alone can advance mankind and that religious beliefs retard the growth of human beings. Secularism understood in this sense is perhaps the basis of Marxism." What has been called "otherwordliness finds no place in this ideology, rather it is inconsistent with it."[35] If tolerance is central to Indian culture and if it is the nearest anticipation of secularism in India, materialism turns out to be the very core of Indian culture. But this is not probably, the correct position. Indian culture may not be altogether otherwordly, but it is not entirely material. The summary rejection of the Carvaka or Lokayata philosophy shows it. Tolerance in Indian culture is basic not because it looked down on religions as obstacles to progress, far from it. It originated out of the high regard for all religions and multifacetedness of truth which each may separately represent. The philosophy of *anekantata* may be said to be the fullest development of the consideration for the many-sidedness of the truth. Tolerance in Indian culture is thus not mere neutrality. It is a positive concept. A secularism based on it would not only bear with all the religions to the extent of political non-interference, but also respect them all by ensuring a harmonious growth of their essence as desired by Asoka. Devoid of this positive aspect the policy of secularism in India is proving a virtual placation of minority religions not unoften with a view to deriving political advantage in the recent democratic set-up Neutrality without understanding and harmonious growth of the essence of all the religions may be good secularism but is only bad tolerance.

This concept of tolerance need not be understood as making the character of Indian culture necessarily otherwordly. Regard for religion is not essentially materially retarding. Religion and materialism are not antithetical. Religion gives man a value-orientation and even material progress cannot be achieved in a value-vacuum. Value-orientation and otherwordliness are not synonymous. Even Marxism is not without a value-frame. Who says Marxism is otherwordly?

Tolerance as a Political Concept

To call the ideal of tolerance in the political sphere of Indian culture a virtue of necessity[36] does not probably reflect a fair evaluation. To say that tolerance had to be practised because India could not develop an efficient system of government through a permanent bureaucracy, is not probably factually correct. Why were the rulers of the Delhi Sultanate, having only a rudimentary administrative set-up, not obliged to practise this virtue of necessity? It may be another thing to conquer and let the conquest go without annexation, like the raids of Mahmud Ghaznavi, or to effect a temporary annexation only to be undone for want of effective administrative and military control, like the conquest of Alexander of India, but it is totally different to conquer with the declaration that the purpose of conquest is merely the assertion of suzerainty for the sake of political unification, and not annexation. This ideal of *dharman-vijaya* is different from that of Asoka who abstained even from taking recourse to arms, and it did not appear in practice before the time of the Guptas. To suggest that the Guptas lacked an efficient administrative set-up and that, in spite of its lasting continuously for, at least, four generations, it was a feat of a militarily controlled state is probably to turn away from historical truth.[37] It is further to be noted that the Arthasastra tradition of elaborate bureaucratic administration had always remained a source of inspiration, even though the actual practice departed from its prescriptions considerably under the stress of circumstances and historical development. It is possible to trace the Arthasastra designation for a few revenue and other officers down to the 12th century and the *niti* authors, like Somadeva, and Candesvara of the 10th and the 13th centuries respectively, were not perpetuating the Arthasastra tradition in vain. In view of these facts, it is not possible to underplay the ideal of tolerance even in the political and military spheres, unless one wants to do it subjectively. At least Europe is not known to have formulated any such ideal even at the height of feudalism which is supposed to be a patent antithesis of the bureaucratic mode of administration. On the contrary, feudal Europe engaged in the adventure of the Crusades which led to the domination of the eastern Mediterranean.[38] Let it be made clear that an ideal may be practised as a virtue of necessity anywhere, but its formulation is always based not so much on the spur of necessity as on the spirit of its culture. Even if its actual practice may be shown to have been at default, its very formulation will always reflect the ethos of its culture.

Tolerance as a Social Concept

Attributing such a broad conception of tolerance to Indian culture as "to you may happen, as you believe" and concluding "that Hinduism is simply not a "religion" in our sense of the word".[39] Max Weber writes, "Hinduism is primarily ritualism, *Dharma*,i.e. "ritualistic duty," which is, according to him, "the central criterion of Hinduism" an offence to which alone leads to deHinduization, and not a mere doctrinal difference which is freely permitted.[40] Ritualism manifests as "every day *dharma* of caste" deriving "its content, in large measure, from the distant past with its taboos, magical norms, and witchcraft" is thus, according to Weber, the essence of Hinduism.[41] This is precisely what Yogendra Singh meant when he called hierarchy the central value of the Indian value-system.[42] Distinction of purity and pollution, taboos, magical norms and witchcraft thus turn out to be the main constituents of the fabric of Indian culture, and nobody is supposed to have bothered about any freedom or liberty taken in the sphere of transcendental formulation so long as this paradise of superstitions, rites and customs at the social level was left undisturbed. In his ostensibly superstitious soil of ritualism or *"dharma"*, was supposedly laid the foundations of caste, which was and still is the only point of admission to the Hindu society.[43] Hence Indian culture is shown to be a queer combination of absolute religious tolerance with an equally extreme social intolerance, and this strange characteristic is taken to be at the root of the development of the social monster known as caste which has got inextricably mixed up with the doctrinaire aspect of Hinduism. This unfortunate turn in India's social development has been held responsible by Weber for preventing her from developing a capitalistic order in spite of all its necessary potential being present in the early stages of her historical growth.[44]

This position originates from the fallacy of imparting totality to an actually partial data. The immense sociological facts and observations released for the first time by the 1911 and subsequent Census Reports have led to a number of broad generalizations. An all time distinction between the normative and factual aspects of the Indian social order was drawn assuming the census data to be factual, and the textual material to be essentially normative, Scholars at once jumped to the conclusion that the picture presented by the census data represents Indian social reality of all times.[45] The 19th and early 20th century historical theory of the stagnant, changeless Indian village community[46] added confidence and validity to the sociologists' attempt to anachronistically attribute, also to the past, the generalization arrived at on the basis of the early 20th century social phenomena. Without taking into account the historical growth and the changes taking place as a result of it, it was credulously believed that what appeared to be the observed essence of the social behaviour in the early 20th century India was also the essence informing social behaviour from the very beginning. Superstitious taboos on contacts, comensality and conubium, and beliefs in the magical efficacy of rites and formulae were regarded as the very spirit of Hinduism. In short, Indian society with such a long history, a glorious civilization with ample written records and monuments to reveal its past was subjected to sociological and anthropological techniques of resurrecting from observation the patterns of life and society of primitive tribes. What is worse is to carry the census observation of 20th century India to the past on the basis of certain prescribed norms of social behaviour which, far from representing these observed social phenomena as facts of ancient Indian life, were only wishful recommendations of the most orthodox section of society bent upon perpetuating its dominance over a larger section of Indian people through indoctrination. Belief in the stagnancy of the Indian social order is, therefore, primary in this approach and, if ever, anything otherwise was endeavoured to be shown on the basis of written records, it was easily dismissed as essentially textual and not based on facts, as if only census data qualified for facts. Identifying the historical with the actual, that too of the recent past, the early 20th century social phenomena of India were proclaimed as something persisting from times immemorial without pausing to think the present is thus ruthlessly taken to the past. If the actual India's social past cannot be known in the manner we have known it in the early 20th century, there is no reason why the latter should be allowed to pass for the former.

Scholars familiar with the Dharmasastra literature would have marked that caste and its rites and rituals, taboos and magic never loom so large on the horizon of this literature as the rules of the *varna* order. Till the time of Manu, there is no sign of the social taboos on food even of the Brahmanas.[47] Castes have been viewed more as a departure from the social norms, than as the rule of the traditional social order.[48] The social frame of reference of the unorthodox salvation religions like Buddhism and Jainism never outrightly condemned the traditional social order as a whole.[49] They only complained of its corruption as an assemblage of rigid, hereditarily determined hierarchy of units which ought to have been based on qualitative distinctions rather than on those of birth and heredity.[50] The elaborately discussed propagation pattern of Hinduism by Weber[51] does not appear to be an all time phenomenon. There is no trace of concocted genealogies or mad race of religious land donations prior to the time of the Guptas. At that time, therefore, the mode of propagation of

Hinduism would have been necessarily different from what has been envisaged by Weber. Indian social history has been a victim of wild generalizations and inaccurate knowledge of sources, seldom studied in their totality. To aggravate the situation further, skills of the anthropologists and sociologists have interposed in the job of historians and the uncalled for prejudices of stagnation and Romanticism have been thrust upon them as models. Things will be clarified only when these issues are explored afresh by the labour of the historians if they approach these problems after disabusing their mind of these befogging idols and drawing a judicious distinction between the old and the new, the normative and the factual. Every age has its own normative and factual aspects. The missing factual aspect of an earlier age should be sought more intensively within the purview of the same and not supplied from our knowledge of the modern epoch, because it is more thorough. Unless that is done, the actual course of India's social history down to the situation prevailing in the early 20th century cannot be reconstructed. But from the broad trends noted above, it may be safely asserted that the birth-based caste distinctions and the social taboos relating to them were not looked upon as positive values till the composition of the classical Dharmasastras. Such things start coming up in the categories of cherished values in the time of the minor Smritis composed after India's encounter with the Arabs.[52]

This is not to suggest that the earlier social order was characterized by the absence of hierarchy. Unlike modern European society, the Indian social order was probably never presented in the frame of egalitarian ideas and values. But just as hierarchical elements characterize European social order, in spite of its egalitarian proclamations,[53] similarly, the ancient Indian social order offered enough scope for egalitarian ideas notwithstanding its hierarchical framework.

It is an account of the gradually contracting scope of such elements with a corresponding growth and increasing rigidity of hierarchical ones that the repeated protests have been made from time to time.[54] The fact that these protests could not effectively break or even relax the progressively tightening net of hierarchical orthodoxy which led to the transformation of *varna* order into the caste-order does not make the finally developed realities of caste-order the central essence of India's social culture. It is, therefore, wrong to call India's social culture as essentially and absolutely intolerant and rigid and to contrast it with the extremely tolerant religious culture attributed to her. The contradiction between the social and religious ethos of ancient India is, therefore, more apparent than real, and is owing to the overlooking of the historical dimension by an overwhelmingly sociological transformation of the historical approach.

To be sure, the nature of her social tolerance was not identical with the modern egalitarian ideals of the West, but it was not as thoroughly hierarchical as is generally supposed on the basis of generalizations based on the data offered by the Census Reports. Socially, Hinduism was not pure ritual and rigidity. *Varna,* not caste was the pivot of her social order and the two were not identical till quite late in her social history.[55] Though not open classes in the European sense of the word, *varnas* were also not rigid and taboo-protected cells like castes. The ideal in respect of them was qualitative rather than hereditary. The lamentable historical phenomenon was their progressive casteification which could not be arrested or reversed. As noted by Setalved and many of us, this sinister process in still on, cramping and transforming beyond recognition our political and educational institutions and processes—the very tools which we picked up from the revolutionary armoury of the modern age to fight it.[56] It is the irony of the historical, sociological and anthropological interpretation that the very cancer which has eaten into the vitals of Indian culture by destroying elements of equality and tolerance in the *varna* order is portrayed as the social genius of it. Tolerance is basic to Indian culture even in the social sphere in the same manner as it is basic to Christianity in its religious sphere. But just as Europe fought a number of religious wars besides passing through the nightmares of savage persecutions in the name of Christianity, similarly, a yet to be fully and historically worked out subjection of the toiling common man of ancient India may be visualized as taking place along lines of the prescriptions of *dharma*—a notorious blend of social customs, ritualism and salvation philosophies. Recourse to violence and social persecution to establish dominance of the elite over the common man divided into a number of castes consigned to different levels of limitation and backwardness ranging down to subhuman levels cannot be ruled out but it appears to have been concealed under the garb of *dharma* systematically substituted in records by a didactic literature preaching increasingly rigid rules of social behaviour. The untold story of India's casteification is perhaps a debt, the historian owes to her common people. If the power-game of the Church was responsible for the one, the lust for the positions of dominance and economic advantage on the part of the Brahmanas acting hand in glove with the Kshatriyas, was responsible for the other. Both the monsters of history originated from a blatant neglect and negation of the spirit of Christianity and Indian culture respectively.

Conclusion

It is now time to ask what is the original Sanskrit, Pali or Prakrit term which embodies the idea of tolerance which we were elucidating so far? One will be surprised to know that there is no word of such an exclusive meaning. It is purely a heuristic trait imposed on Indian culture by an observer. We have yet to find the original expression approaching the concept elaborated above. Perhaps the intrinsic ethos is this significant discovery wich would mitigate the air of externality involved in the whole exercise. It is surprising that the custodians of esoteric wisdom of this culture which is no longer a sealed book to us, did not debate or spell out such a key concept as tolerance and, owing to their silence, we are obliged to guess even the right word for it, as if, from the mute remains of Harappa and Mohenjodaro. Perhaps, we trust our observation more than our initiation into the valued traditions of the culture we are trying to study.

We no doubt come across words like *sahatva*[57], *ksanti*[58], *ksama*[59], *titlksa*[60], etc., in the list of traditional virtues but they carry the sense of sufferance, forbearance, forgiveness and endurance, respectively. For religious tolerance Asoka appears to use the expression *saravadhi,* i.e. the growth of essence[61] which hardly bears the notion of disapproval or refraining from persecution associated with the concept of tolerance as its meaning. The only word approaching marginally the sense of persecution is *parapasanda garha,* i.e. censuring of others' faith.[62] According to Monier Williams, this censure is limited to disgust expressed in speech only. Asoka says that even speaking ill of others' faith for the glorification of one's own damages one's own faith.

The word which appears to include all aspects of the multifaceted concept of tolerance discussed above is *ahimsa*[63] or non-violence. Though negatively spelled, *ahimsa* is traditionally supposed to be the mother of all the virtues and includes much more than the concept of tolerance. The purpose of the element of negation in this word is not to make it a word of negative meaning denoting merely abstention from violence, but to make it all-inclusive, so that no form of violence may escape through the inadequacies of a positive characterization. It is like negation of the wilful negation of life, i.e. *ahimsa* in this respect and is hence a form of the most positive characterization.[64] This is why *ahimsa* is the source of all other virtues which constitute the universal religion (*sadharana dharma*) of mankind. Such a basic culture is said to be the essential condition for the growth of religious consciousness without which one is sub-religious, i.e. incapable of being religious at all.[65]

The positive constituents of *ahimsa* in the present context appear to be *daya, dana, sarya, aparigraha, maitri, karuna, bhutahita,* etc. Of these, *daya, karuna* and *maitri* stand for fellow-feeling, sympathy and compassion. As persons advocating a different faith or following a different social order or set of values are also human beings, *daya, karuna,* or *maitri* expected of us as natural should prevent any violence to them on any level. There is no question of refraining from violence, for violence in this case is not natural. It is the most unnatural thing. Any violence is also prevented by the centrality of *satya* or *truth* common to all of them up to a certain level at least beyond which the *anekantata* of truth renders conflict unnecessary. As it is the most natural duty of each to support the truth even at the cost of one's interest, *dana* or liberality becomes the *terra firma* of all religions. The householder is often compared with a pond to whom every religious organization turns for sustenance. The same laity supported, by its liberality, the propagators of different faiths and, for the level of laity, the teachings of all the religions were common. Asoka asks his people to be liberal both to the Brahmanas and Sramanas. *Aparigraha* is the virtue of honesty in possession so that there should not be grabbing of liberality or cases of forced liberality. Lastly, *bhutahita* is supposed to be the aim of all adjustments and endeavour.[66] The author of the *Mahabharata* declares from the house top, whether nobody listens to him, that doing good to others, (*paropakara*) leads to virtue (*punya*) and inflicting pain on others (*parapidanam*) leads to vice (*papa*).[67] There is no better reward for the labours of a truly religious man than his satisfaction of removing the grievances of suffering humanity.[68] Traditional roots of tolerance thus go deeper than those of its conception merely as an observed fact. In the traditional scheme of things, *ahimsa,* including a number of virtues besides tolerance in the broadest sense, constitutes the infrastructure of all religious and social institutions. The apparent abrogation of this principle in the social sphere is not a perverse quality of Indian culture, but its historical failure. Caste is by no means a valued creation of this culture and it does not represent the ideology of its social order. It is a corruption and degenerate distortion of the *varna* system like the slave, the serf or the proletariat of the Graeco-Roman feudal and capitalistic social orders.

Resistance to caste is noticed throughout the course of history, but in ever receding and weakening tones till it degenerates into the heuristically recognized value of transcendence in the *Ramacaritamanasa* of Tulasidasa. Unlike Karna who fights for his right of equality, Sugriva, Vibhisana, Nisada and Sabari are redeemed from their wretched social destiny by the transcendental divine grace falling on them. In their case the wall of social discrimination breaks because of divine intervention which is all powerful and above all kinds of rules and laws. Their freedom from the iron rigidity of caste is not claimed as a matter of right. There can be no greater stultification of resistance to social injustice than this. But to give even this weak expression to the sentiment of social freedom, while yet advocating with all the vigour the rigidity of caste distinctions, reconciling the contradiction involved with the myth of transcendence, is a clear enough sign that the spirit of Indian culture did not quietly submit to the destiny of the inevitable even during the darkest days of its subversion for vested interest. It is high time to systematically plan and execute the casting away of caste and restore to our social order the traditional foundations of *ahimsa* or tolerance characteristic of Indian culture.

NOTES AND REFERENCES

1. Gazo, Ernest Wolf. 'Zusammenhang mit dem Bedeutungswandel des Worktes Kultur' *Meisenneim Glan: Verlag Anton Hain,* Vol. X, 1974, p. 119.
2. *International Encyclopaedia of Social Sciences* (*IESS*), Vol. 6, p. 358.
3. Om Prakash, "Concept of Hierarchy and Power in the Ancient Indian Theory of Social and State", *Proceedings of the Indian History Congress,* XL Session, Waltair, 1979, pp. 46-56.
4. Ibid., pp. 49-50, 54.
5. Om Prakash, "Inherent Historical Pattern and Modern Conceptual Frameworks", A paper presented to the 1982 Seminar on 'Battle for Ideologies' organized by Vikas Parisad, New Delhi, January 9-11.
6. "We should learn to view life from a historical point of view before we can realize the value of culture." Munshi, K.M., *Foundations of India Culture,* Bombay, 1974, p. 3.
7. Om Prakash, "Systems, History and the Question of Perspective" in Devahuti (ed.), *Historical and Political Perspectives,* pp. 8-9.
8. For details of allegations on Indian Culture by Archer and its defence by Ghose, Aurobindo, *Foundation of Indian Culture,* pp. 108 ff.
9. Coomaraswamy, "What has India Contributed to Human Welfare" in *Dance of Siva,* pp. 22-27.
10. Panikkar, K.M., *Essential Features of Indian Culture,* Bombay, 1964, pp. 5-30.
11. Munshi, op. cit. pp. 73-76.

12. *Encyclopaedia of Religion and Ethics (ERE)*, Vol. 12, p. 361.
13. Ibid., p. 360.
14. Basham, A.L. *The Indian Subcontinent in Historical Perspective*, London, 1958, pp. 11-12.
15. Max Weber cited in Donald Eugene Smith, *India as a Secular State*, pp. 61-62.
16. Setalvad, M.C., *Secularism*, Patel Memorial Lecture, 1965, Government of India Publications, 1967, p. 12.
17. Munshi, op. cit., p. 72; Radhakrishnana, S., *The Hindu View of Life*, London, 1963, pp. 83-88.
18. Munshi, op. cit., p. 72.
19. Panikkar, op. cit., p. 45.
20. Setalvad, op. cit., p. 25.
21. "...........early Indian society was as aquisitive as are the societies of present-day Europe and America", Basham, op. cit., p. 19.
22. Singh, Yogendra, *Essays on Modernization in India*, p. 179.
23. Ibid., p. 180.
24. *Supra*, p. 67.
25. "Perry Anderson links Rome's political and military expansionism with the mode of production which collapsed when the imperical frontiers ceased to advance." *Passages From Antiquity to Feudalism*, London, 1975, p. 93.
26. *ERE*, Vol. XII, p. 361.
27. Ibid.
28. There are a few instances of religious conflicts in Indian history, as for example the persecution of Buddhists by Pusyamitra Sunga. L.B. Kenny also draws our attention to some such incidents between Saivas and Vaisnavas in South India (Presidential Address to the XXIV Session of the Indian History Congress, Chandigarh, 1973). But these instances are mere exceptions rather than the rule.
29. *ERE*, Vol. XII, p. 363.
30. Ibid.
31. "Denouncing the execution of Servetus, he (Castello) argued that, if the end of Christianity be the diffusion of a spirit of beneficence, persecution must be its extreme antithesis, and that, if persecutin can be the essential element of a religion, the religion must be a curse to humanity, Ibid., p. 363.
32. Cited in Ibid., p. 365.

33. Weber, *Religion of India,* Illinois, 1958, p. 23.
34. Radhakrishnan, op. cit., p. 27.
35. Setalvad, op. cit., p. 28.
36. *Supra,* p. 6.
37. Independent works have been published on Gupta administration, e.g. Dikshitar, V.R.R., *Gupta Polity.*
38. Anderson, Perry, *Passages from Antiquity to Feudalism,* p. 193.
39. Weber, op. cit., p. 23.
40. Ibid., p. 24.
41. Ibid., p. 25.
42. Ibid., p. 57 f.
43. Weber, op. cit., pp. 9-21.
44. In fact his whole work is devoted to the inquiry of this inhibiting social factor as is clear from his following statement at the beginning of his book *Religion in India* (p. 4); "Here we shall inquire as to the manner in which Indian religion, as one factor among many, may have prevented capitalistic development (in the Occidental sense)."
45. Srinivas and Shah, op. cit., p. 358. (*IESS,* Vol. 6).
46. An expression of the popular version of the theory may be seen in the following statement of Humayun Kabir: "In spite of the many changes in kings and kingdoms, the organized social life of the community has hardly changed in the last two or three thousand years.The village republics which were established in India in early times are in one sense extant to this day." *The Indian Heritage,* p. 46.
47. Om Prakash, "Social Implications of the Restrictions on the Acceptability of food for Brahmanas in Manu", *Proceedings of the Indian History Congress,* XLI Session, Bombay 1981, pp. 161-167.
48. Traditionally the origin of caste has been explained through irregular mixed marriages not sanctioned by the law of the *varnas,* Kane, P.V., *History of Dharmasastra,* Vol. II, Part I, pp. 5 ff.
49. Weber, op. cit., p. 20.
50. *Dighanikaya,* I, pp. 104-5.
51. Weber, op. cit., pp. 9-21.
52. Sharma, B.N., *Social Life in Northern India,* Delhi 1966, p. 36. He makes an extensive use of the provisions of minor *smritis*

in bringing out the rapidly growing rigidity of the caste system.

53. "Modern industrial societies are both egalitarian in aspiration and hierarchical in organization." Aron. R., *Progress and Disillusion,* Pall Mall Press, 1968, p. XV. "It is not that inequality among men has ceased to exist but only the context in which it exists has been altered." Beteille, Andre, *Inequality Among Men,* Blackwell, Oxford, 1977, p. 149.
54. These protests are registered through a number of epic stories, Jainism, Buddhism and a number of other religious movements like Vaisanavism, Lingayatism, Kabirpantha, Aryasamaja, etc.
55. Senart, E., *Caste in India,* Delhi, 1977, p. 129.
56. *Supra,* pp. 67 f. According to Weber, "....religious movements of expressly anti-Brahmanical and anti-caste character, that is, contrary to one of the fundamentals of Hinduism, have been in all essentials returned to caste order." op. cit., p. 19.
57. Monier Williams refers to its occurrence in *Kamandakiya Nitisara, Rajatarangini* and *Kathasaritasagara, Sanskrit-English Dictionary,* p. 1193.
58. *Manu,* V. 107.
59. *Atharvaveda,* XII. 1. 29: *Ramayana,* II. 35, 31; III. 49, 25.
60. *Atharvaveda,* XII. 1. 48: *Panini,* I. 2. 20; *Manu,* IX. 161; *Visnu Purana,* I. 7. 1-53.
61. Rock Edict, XII, Sircar, D.C., *Select Inscriptions,* Vol. I, p. 32.
62. Ibid., p. 33.
63. For references to Ahimsa see Walli, Koshelya, *Ahimsa in Indian Thought,* Varanasi, 1974, pp. 34-57.
64. Nikam, N.A., *Some Concepts of Indian Culture,* Simla, 1973, p. 31.
65. Cf. Singh, R., *Dharma ki Hindu Avadharna,* Allahabad, 1977, pp. 76 ff.
66. Cf. Dandekar, R.N., *Insights into Hinduism,* Delhi, 1979, pp. 102-104: Singh, R., op. cit., pp. 69-88 ; Pandey, R.B., *Bharatiya Niti ka Vikasa,* Patna, 1965, p. 121.
67. *Astadasa puranesu vyasasya vacanam dvayam, parokakarah punyaya papaya parapidanam.*
68. *Natyaham kamaye rajyam na svargam na punarbhavam, kamaye dukkhataptanam praninamartinasanam.*

7

Plagiarism and Prejudices in Indica

U.P. Arora

Megasthenes had stayed and seen more in India than any other Greek traveller. Like the companions of Alexander, he was not obliged to take his notes "on the run" and so could be a patient observer. But, despite being in this advantageous position, he did not make the most of his opportunities and we notice that many of his statements are of negative value. By his stay in India he was not led to distrust the fabulous descriptions of his predecessors. The unreliable character of his report was not digestible even to ancient readers for the authors like Strabo[1] and Plin[2] had greatly disparaged his accounts. In his description of India, Megasthenes went to the extent of transferring even the legends of Homer and Pindar, to Indian soil. He located India as a venue of Homer's myth of the fight of Pygmies against the Cranes and partridges only adding verisimilitude by the detail that Cranes had been found later, with the points of miniature weapons still embedded in their flesh.[3] The long-lived Hyperborean's of Pindar were also shifted to India by Megasthenes.[4] Megasthenes took much material from Herodotus. As he probably thought on general grounds that he should prefer Herodotus to Ktesias, gold guarding Griffins[5] in order to support Herodotus's gold digging ants.[6]

Megasthenes's description of the tribes who cohabited with their women in public and ate the bodies of the dead relatives[7] was from Herodotus.[8] His division of the Indians into seven classes, i.e. philosophers *(philosophoi)* or sophists *(sophistai),* formers *(georgo);* herdsmen *(boukolo, poimenes, nomees)* and hunters *(thereutai);* artisans *(tekhnitai)* labourers *(ergazomenoi)* and tradesmen *(kapelikoi);* warrior *(polemisrai),* overseers *(ephorio)* and superintendents *(epislopoi)* and councillors *(symbouloi)*[9] correspond with Herodotus's seven classes of Egypt.[10] As Megasthenes's division of Indian society is not in conformity with Indian sources, it appears that he evolved his own seven classes having Herodotus's seven classes of Egypt in mind. The Greek authors had continually drawn analogies between Egypt and India from the time of Alexander's expedition.[11]

Next to Herodotus, may be mentioned Ktesias in whose account of the fabulous Indian races, a great interest was shown by Megasthenes. The interest in marvels was prevalent in classical works on India from the very beginning. Skylax, the very first Greek traveller and author on India, who could write more on his experience of descending the Indus took interest in amazing his readers with spicy material.[12] Ktesias's book on India is, in its present form full of mythical tales. Relying on such gossip, Megasthenes too believed in the existence of one foot men *(okvpodas)*, one-eyed men *(Monommatous),* men with enormous ears[13] *(Enotoloitas)* and barking men *(Caninis)*[14] of India. It is lamentable that the one who had closely watched the Indian affairs himself, took material from Ktesias who was never in India and had based his work on hearsay stories of soldiers and travellers only. Megasthenes's account of the people who lived only for forty years[15] was from Ktesias.[16] His description of the ferocious Indian dogs who could capture even lions[17] and single-horned horses[18] may also be traced back to Ktesias's *Indika*.[19] Following Ktesias,[20] he believed the historicity of mythical queen Samiramis, but improved upon him by refuting the account of her confrontation with the Indians. Megasthenes reported that no attempt was made by Semiramis to fight against the Indians.[21] Megasthenes knew the recent literature of Alexander's companions as well. From Alexander's surveyor Baeton[22] he took the account of "feet reversed wild men" and interestingly enough, gave the same reason to explain why certain savages had never been brought before Sandrocottus.[23] Following Alexander's followers,[24] Megasthenes too rejected the Persian invasion on India and accepted only the myth of Dionysus and Herakles's campaigns in India before Alexander.[25] Megasthenes draws our attention to some grain *bosporon*[26] which cannot be clearly identified. Before him it was mentioned as a product of India by Onesicritus only.[27] The statement that Indian elephants were larger than those of Africans was also borrowed by Megasthenes,[28] from Onesicritus. In his attempt of idealizing Indians, Megasthenes was greatly inspired by Onescritus's narrative of India and of Mousicanos. The absence of slavery, law-suits, and formal contracts, which marked as characteristics features of the people of Mousicanos,[29] were generalized for the whole of India by Megasthenes.[30] Likewise, the regard for beauty, which was an attribute of the people of Katha state in India of Onesicritus,[31] became a characteristics of Indians in general in the account of Megasthenes.[32] Onesicritus's theme of emphasizing austere life of the Indians despite having everything in abundance,[33] also echoes in Megasthenes.[34] In fact Megasthenes adopted Onesicritus to suit his own purposes, but whereas Onesicritus had the skill of combining his observation with imagination, Megasthenes lacked that. It is easy to draw the line in

Megasthenes between serious, if not always accurate, accounts of custom and sensational reports of strange things. Megasthenes's idealized pictures of the Indians carry many such points which may be seen in Plato's description of Atlantis,[35] Euhmerus's Panchaea,[36] and Hecataeus's Egypt.[37] Wearied from the gross materialism economic uncertainties, and imperial ambitions of their ages, these Greeks visualized the land of their ideal in distant places like Egypt and India or in the lands of their imagination like Atlantis and Panchaea. The theme *aboriente lux* which more frequently heard in the Hellenistic age, led to emphasize the origin of civilization in Egypt. Hecatalus of Abdera wrote a book *Aegvptiaka* in order to establish the supremacy of Egypt. Megasthenes's *Indika* seems to have been written as a direct reply to *Aegyptiaka,* for he modelled his *Indika* on the method, form, and content of Hecataeus's work. The *Indika* is a systematic account of Indian culture with geography, flora, fauna, people mythology, history, etc. It appears to show that "India is an even better land than Hecataeus's Egypt, a Platonic ideal state with philosophers on the top and that all civilizations spring from India and not Egypt."[38]

Thus the statement that all the land in India belonged to the king, was probably from Ptolemaic Egypt. In the names used in connection with state administration, the external influences can be clearly recognized. The use of *dioikesis* (Department of Finance) and *dioketas* (Chief Financial Official) are more reminiscent of Hellenistic Egypt than Greek usage and this is shown also by the name *Nomarkhoi* (chiefs of provinces) which was purely an Egyptian institution). The office attending foreigners was probably reminiscent of Greek *Proxenoi* and *Proxema* which performed similar duties at Sparta and at Elis.[40] Megasthenes's *agronomo*[41], who were represented as in-charge of land including its cultivation and irrigation may be traced in the works of Plato[42] and Aristotle.[43] Likewise, the reference to milestones in Megasthenes may be of Persian or Egyptian origin.[44] It is true that Megasthenes repeated many of the statements of his predecessors without acknowledging or recognizing them, but at some places he also contradicted their statements. For example, Megasthenes informed that the Indians were wearing coloured embroidered clothes,[45] but Strabo draws our attention towards the historians, who had written that Indians in general wore white linen or cotton garments.[46] Whereas Alexander's companion Nearchus spoke about the hand-woven linen clothes as writing material of the Indians.[47] Megasthenes reported that the writing was completely unknown in India.[48] The elephants were seen as the possession of many rich men by Nearchus,[49] but Megasthenes commented that no private man in India was allowed to keep elephants.[50]

It is possible that the area visited by Megasthenes might have represented certain things, which were contrary to the reports of Alexander's companions, and so probably, Megasthenes draws our attention deliberately to pinpoint that. But his remark that the Indians were ignorant of writing and regulated everything by memory is strange, when we remember the vast mass of literature long before the arrival of Megasthenes. That epistolary correspondence was perfectly usual in the time of Megasthenes is evidenced by the *Arthasastra*.[51] Megasthenes's predecessor Nearchus was well aware of the existence of writing in India. Megasthenes could not possibly have been ignorant of this fact, since he was in India for a considerable period. It is notable that in some of his other statements one notices the references to writing.[52] It may be observed here that since in the context of their unwritten laws, the truth seems to be in the case of judicial transaction only. The ancient Indian law texts, known as Smriti literature were the laws which were memorized. Thus what Megasthenes said might have been that the Indians did not employ written laws because the judges knew the law by heart.

There are so many references to the system of slavery in the Smriti literature[53] and other Indian texts that it is difficult to accept its absence. It is further to be noted that the reason for the existence of polygamous practice among the Brahmanas was attributed by Megasthenes to the absence of slavery among them. According to him since the Brahmanas did not have slaves, they married many wives to have more, children around them to attend to their wants.[54] If there was a complete absence of slavery in India the specific reference to Brahmanas would not be necessary. It appears that in his enthusiasm for idealizing Indians the statement made by Onesicritus for the people of Mousicanos[55] was generalized by Megasthenes for the Indians in general. Some of Megasthenes's observations which appear to be at variance with Indian literature may be due to misunderstanding of the foreign traveller. Thus the report that only the king could have horses and elephants may be due to some reports which stated that these animals "were a royal mount". Similar errors of interpretation may be behind his report that all the land in India belonged to the king.[56] Likewise, when Megasthenes stated that the wise man who had prophesied falsely was condemned to silence for the rest of his life,[57] he had probably in mind the distorted idea of the vow of silence taken by the munis. It was a foreign traveller like Megasthenes, within a short period of his stay. In his interpretation of Indian things he must also have been hampered by the language difficulty. We are reminded of a series of dialogues between Onesicritus and the Indian philosophers, where the necessity for using a series of interpreters greatly impeded his enquiries.[58]

In some instances the fragments of Megasthenes as preserved by Arrian and Strabo, contradict each other. For example, in Strabo's version of Megasthenes it was said that the tombs of the Indians were simple and the mounds raised over them very small,[59] but Arrian reported complete absence of such tombs.[60] In the same way while Strabo's rendering of Megasthenes stated that any profession was open to a sophist.[61] Arrian quoted that anyone could become a sophist.[62] Perhaps the original report was that a change of class was not permitted "except in the case of the philosophers", which would at least be an explanation of the contradiction. Such contradictions were probably on account of the error made by the copyists, as Megasthenes's work has not reached us directly.

Thus we see that while the Greek envoy had ample opportunity, so far as we know, to give a fair picture of what he saw, there are many circumstances that would tend to obscure this picture. Compared with Herodotus's travel to Egypt we notice that Megasthenes went into India under some-what similar circumstances. Like Herodotus, he had some ideas in his head of what he would find there, and like him Megasthenes was dependent on interpreters. But unlike Herodotus, he was not so investigative for the things which already had previous Greek accounts. When Herodotus visited Egypt, he reported certain matters on the basis of his own observation *(opsis)*, others as known to him only by 'hearsay' *(akoe)*. This 'hearsay' as told by his informants in Egypt was further investigated by him, whenever possible. Megasthenes, on the other hand, never did this. His observation of the life around him qualifies him as a journalist; it does not show that he was a historian, for it implies no ability to evaluate conflicting testimonies.[63]

Despite Megasthenes's unreliable character, the classical literature on India was greatly influenced by him. The classical view of India did not improve upon Megasthenes and the authors like Diodorus Siculus, Arrian and Strabo, derived their knowledge of India mainly from him. It is unfortunate that these authors did not take advantage of their contemporary reports, which were more reliable. They were obtained as a result of increased trade of the Graeco-Roman world with south India. A regular trade route was in continuance between parts of the Persian Gulf and India along the route taken by Nearchus and his fleet and for at least half a century Roman merchants had trade directly with India, using the monsoon to sail from the Red Sea of the East Coast of the subcontinent. But none of this filters into the works of these authors and their accounts remained resolutely traditional. When Arrian repeated the statement of Megasthenes that only Alexander had made an expedition to India,[64] he did not consider Seleucus I, Antiochus I, the Parthians, or the Kushanas and so his work was in no sense an account of India in Roman times. It was not so that the new information could not be known by the authors of the Graeco-Roman age, when thousands of Greek sailors had made the annual passage from Egypt to India and many Greek soldiers, merchants, and craftsman had worked in South India. The frequent vessels going to India were well-known to these authors[65] and it is curious to note that while writing about other foreign lands, they did refer to the late Hellenistic as well as the reports reaching through commercial intercourse, but in the case of India, such information was used only sporadically.[66] The information brought by the sailors returning from India was taken by the educated Greeks as non-serious. Strabo considered these sailors stupid, from whom serious reports could hardly be expected.[67] Dio-Chrysostomos, a Stoic-Cynic wanderer, too disparaged them, for their information was not in accordance with his romantic imagination of India.[68] The text *Periplus of the Erythraean Sea* by an unknown author and Ptolemy's *Geography* did use extensively the reports of sailors but they were more concerned with Mathematical Geography—i.e. ascertaining the true locations of places—than with descriptions of land and people, which had chiefly interested Megasthenes and other authors in the classical tradition. The text *Periplus of the Erythraean Sea* and Ptolemy's *Geography* were not serious works according to the classical yardstick for, unlike Megasthenes and Alexander's companions, they lacked literary merit and elegance of style. Likewise, the new information supplied by Christian missionaries Clement, of Alexandra[69] St. Jerome[70], and Archelaos[71] too did not belong to the classical tradition. In a mine written in the Graeco-Roman age there are references to South India.[72]

From the above discussion we should not discredit the account of Megasthenes completely. When Greek writers before Megasthenes have described any part of India, Megasthenes tends to accept the account that seems most plausible, contenting himself with minor modifications, but where he had no earlier work to guide him and was forced to supplement his own impressions by interrogating Indians, his account is trustworthy. For instance, when he was forced to work on a description of the Ganges and its tributaries[73] without some earlier work to guide him, he seems to have acquainted himself reasonably well. But when he gets away from the part of India he knows, he is only as reliable as the source he follows, and we cannot be sure he is following the best source. Our evaluation of Megasthenes reveals that for his description of India, he took extensive material from previous Greek authors. The Greek prejudices were greatly dominant in him. So, it is imperative that in order to corroborate Megasthenes's report, along with the Indian evidences, the classical background should also be studied by Ideologists. This applies to all classical authors on India. The study of their classical background has been neglected so far. Only after the analysis of both Indian and classical evidences, can we obtain some fruitful results.

NOTES AND REFERENCES

1. Strabo, II, 1, 9.
2. Pliny, *Natural History,* VI 58 (soln, 52, 3).
3. Megasthenes in F. Jacoby's *Die Fragments der griechischen Historiker* (Berlin 1923) No. 715, F. 27b (Strabo, XV, I, 57).
4. Ibid.
5. Ktesias, Jac, No. 688, F. 45 (26, phot., Bib., 75, 46b).
6. Herod. III, 102-105.
7. Meg., F. 27b, Strabo, XV, I, 56).
8. Herod., III, 99, 101.
9. F. 7 (Diod, II, 40-41), F. 19a (Arr. Ind., 11-12) F. 19b (Strabo, XV, I, 39-41, 45, 46-49).
10. Herodotus (II, 164) had divided the people of Egypt into seven classes of priests *(Irees),* soldiers *(Machimoi),* Herdsmen *(Boukoloi),* swineherds *(Subotai),* tradesmen *(Kapeloi),* Interpreters *(Etmenees),* and steersmen*(Kubernetai).*
11. See U.P. Arora, India vis-à-vis Ehtiora-Egypt in Classical Accounts, *Graeco-Arabica,* Vol. I, 1982, Athens.
12. Scylax, Jac, No. 709, F. 6, 7a, F. 7b.
13. F. 27b (Strabo; XV, I, 57).
14. Megasthenes in C., Mueller's *Fragmenta Historicarum Graecarum* (Paris, 1856), Vol. II, p. 424, Frag. 31 (Pliny, N.H., VII. 2. 14), Frag. 32 (Solin, 52, 26), Schwanbeck's Frag. No. 30 and 30b, Jacoby does not include this passage in Megasthenes's work.
15. Jacoby, No. 715, F. 13a (Arrian, Ind., IX, 17).
16. Ktes, Jac, No. 688, F. 52 (Pling, N.H. 7, 29).
17. F. 21a (Strabo, XV, 1, 37).

18. F. 27b (Strabo, XV, 1, 56).
19. Ktes., F. 45(10, Phot, Bib., 72, 45b); F. 45 (45, phot., Bib. 72, 48a).
20. Ktes., F. 1b (Diod, S.K., II, 16-20, 22).
21. F. 11a (Strabo, XV, 1, 6).
22. Baiton, Jac, No. 119, F. 5 (Pliny, N.H., VII, 11).
23. Meg., F. 27b (Strabo, XV, 1, 57).
24. Aristoblus, Jac, No. 139, F. 55 (Arrians *Anab.*, VI, 3, 4); Nearchus, Jac., No. 133, F. 32 (Arrian, *Anab*, VI, 3, 4) See W.W. Taru, *Alexander the Great* (Camp, 1948) Vol. II, pp. 55-63.
25. F. 14 (Arrian, Ind, IX, 9-10); F. 12a (Strato, XV, 1, 6-7); F. 11b (Arr. Ind., V. 4-7).
26. F. 4 (Diod, Sic, II, 354).
27. Onesic, Jac, No., 134, F. 15 (Strabo, XV, 1, 18).
28. F. 4 (Diod. Sic., II, 354).
29. On Sic., Jac. No. 134, F. 24 (Strabo, XV, 1, 34).
30. Meg., F. 32 (Strabo, XV, 1, 54); F. 16 (Arr., Ind., X. 8); F. 32 (Strabo, XV, 1, 53).
31. Onesic., F. 21 (Strabo, XV, 1, 30).
32. F. 32 (Strabo, XV, 1, 54).
33. Onesic., F. 24 (Strabo, XV, 1, 34).
34. For the Wealth of the Indians: F.4 (Diod., Sic., II, 36); F. 32 (Strabo, XV, 1, 53-54).
35. Plato *Critias,* 111-120.
36. Jacoby, No. E3, F. 2 (Diod., VI, 1, 5-9), F. 3 (Diod, V, 41-46).
37. Jacoby's Fragments, Vol. III, No. 264.
38. Murray, *Classical Quarterly,* Vol. XXII (1972), p. 208).
39. Meg. F. 19a (Arrian, Ind. XII), See Otto Stein, *Megasthenes and Kautilaya* (Akademie der Wiessenschaften in Wien, Band 191, 1922), pp. 192-3.
40. See Vincent Smith, 'Consular Offices in India and Greece' *Indian Antiquary,* XXXIV, 200.
41. Meg., F. 31 (Strabo, XV, 1, 50).
42. Plato, *Leges,* VI, 760B ff., VIII, 8434 844B, 848E; IX, 873E, 881C.
43. Aristotle, *Politics,* 1321b 30; 1331b 15.
44. Meg, F. 31 (Strabo, XV, 1, 50), Stein, op. cit., p. 246.
45. Meg, F. 32 (Strabo, XV, 1, 54).

46. Strabo, XV, 1, 71.
47. Nearchus, Jac., No. 133, F. 33 (Strabo, XV, 1, 67).
48. Meg, F. 32 (Strabo, XV, 1, 53).
49. Nearchus, F. 11 (Arr. *Ind.*, XVII, 2), F. 22 (Strabo, XV, 1, 43).
50. Meg, F. 19b (Strabo, XV, 1, 41).
51. *Arth.* II. 10.
52. For example, in F. 19b (Strabo, XV, 1, 30) is mentioned the great Synod, in which at the beginning of the new year the philosophers were bringing forward in public their written statements with reference to the affairs connected with the state. In F. 31 ((Strabo, XV, 1, 50) pillars are mentioned showing the distances, which again prove the existence of writing.
53. See *Manusmriti* (VIII, 415), where seven kinds of slaves were cited. Also see *Manu,* IV, 180, 185, 253-256; VIII 66, 70, 363, 416-17; IX. 55; *Yajnavalka* II, 182-83; *Nerada,* V. 26-43.
54. Meg, F. 33 (Strabo, XV, 1, 59).
55. Onesic. F. 24 (Strabo, XV, 1, 34).
56. Meg, F. 19b (Strabo, XV, 1, 40); F. 4 (Diod. II, 40.
57. Meg, F. 19b (Arr., Ind., XI, 5); F. 19b (Strabo, XV, 1, 39.
58. Onesic. F. 17a (Strabo, XV, 1, 64).
59. Meg, F. 32 (Strabo, XV, 1, 54).
60. Meg, F. 15 (Arr., Ind., X. 1).
61. F.19a (Strabo, XV, 1, 49).
62. Meg, F. 19a (Arr., Ind., XII, 8-9).
63. See T.S. Brown, *American Journal of Philology,* (Vol. 76, 1955), pp. 18-33.
64. Arrian, *Indika,* V, 4-7.
65. See Strabo, II, 5, 12; Lucian, *Hermotimus,* 4.
66. See A. Dihle, "The Conception of India in Hellenistic and Roman Literature", *Proceedings of the Cambridge Philological Association,* CXC (n.s. 10, 19(4).
67. Strabo, XV, 1, 4.
68. Dio Chry, *O, atlones,* XXXV, 22-23.
69. Clem, Alex, *Sromatels,* I, 154, 71-72; III, 7, 60.
70. St. Jerome (Hieronymus), *Contra Jov. Epist.* 1, 2, 26.
71. Archelacs, *Archelal et. Menetis Disputatio,* I, 97.
72. See D.L. Page, *Greek Literary Papyri* (Loeb series), 336 ff..
73. Meg, F. 9 (Arrian, *Ind.*, IV, 36.

8

Land Grants to Brahmanas in Early India: A Critical Analysis

R.P. Tripathi

Land grants may be broadly classified into two groups:

- Villages any plots of land made over to the Brahmanas and religious institutions—monasteries and temples.
- Grants made by way of rewards, gifts or maintenance of certain individuals—the members of royal clans, relatives, warriors chiefs and officers.

There is a mass of inscriptional and literary evidence to show that the former type of land grants were issued for the explicit purpose of the spiritual welfare of the donors and their ancestors with little positive secular obligation on the donees. The Dharmasastra literature contains numerous references highlighting the importance of gifts in general and land gifts in particular as compared to other rites.[1] Manu holds that instead of throwing the edibles into the fire, one should put them into the mouth of a Brahmana and elaborates it further by saying that one who bestows a gift on a Brahmana, versed in the Vedas, reaps the most coveted fruit.[2] In fact, dana is capable of bestowing all blessings on the donor if he gives generously for the fulfilment of his desires. He states that different articles of dana entitle him for the fulfilment of different desires.[3] For instance, by giving gold one is gifted with a long life but by giving land he will enjoy the earth.[4] Significantly enough, gifts of gold, silver and houses are subordinated to the gift of land as the latter is placed first in order of enumeration.[5] Yajnavalkya also gives top priority to the gift of land compared to the gifts of gold and other items as it certainly entitles the donor for the reward of enjoyment of heaven.[6] He advises the donee not to reject the gift of land if it is offered to him.[7] Though gifts of cows, land and Saraswati are said to be superior to any other gift and are called *atidana*.[8] Land gifts are said to have surpassed all other gifts in the Mahabharata[9] and the Vishnudharmottara Purana.[10] Devala[11] speaks of three main categories of things that can be subjects of gifts and the gift of land occurs in the first category along with gold and cows. Gifts of certain important objects including land are called *mahadana*.[12] That land gift was considered the most valuable gift is attested by the epigraphs of the Imperial Guptas and their successors.[13] But it appears that the practice of offering land-gifts to the Brahmanas was limited to different royal houses, their feudatories and wealthy persons only. The common man could hardly afford giving land as *dana* owing to poverty and limited resources.

The purpose of granting lands to Brahmanas has been a subject of debate among different groups of scholars. The sources at our disposal speak in one voice that grants to holy and learned Brahmanas were made in order to acquire *punya* (merit) in this world as well as in the next world for the donors, their ancestors and descendants. But some scholars have not taken the statement at its face value and have suggested some concealed motives behind the land grants made over to temples and to Brahmanas. They have emphasized the needs, circumstances and class interests or social compulsions while analyzing the causative factors behind the whole scheme of land grants. To quote M.G.S. Narayanan: "The class interest that was served by land grants was that of the Brahmin-courtiers-cum landlords—a group which exhibited insatiable land hunger through the centuries. It was collective and conscious action on the part of the group appearing in different roles that produced an unending series of land grants in India. The kings who formally granted land were merely instrumental in achieving this objective."[14] Other reasons pointed out by him in this regard are kings' weakness for praise and fear of guilt, etc. But it is most likely the result of the desire of the rulers to muster the support of a class which was influential and highly respected in society owing to its vast learning, religious temperament and spiritual leadership. As they wielded moral influence on the native population, the ruling class preferred to gain their favour for retaining power and also for ensuring the well-being of its descendants. It was almost impossible to govern the kingdom without the help and support of the Brahmanas. The learned Brahmanas were capable of averting or diffusing the revolt of the masses against the kings and their allies. A perpetual bond between the rulers and the ruled was effected with the help of the Brahmanas. The power of wisdom and diplomacy of the Brahmanas helped in a big way in running the administrative machinery of the kingdom.

The question arises as to what type of land was considered ideal for the purpose of gifts to Brahmanas and religious institutions? The literary evidences do not approve of all kinds of land suitable for *dana*. Lakshmidhara[15] quotes several passages from *Brhaspati, Nandi Purana, Aditya Purana* and the *Mahabharata* which reveal that the land meant for *dana* to Brahmanas and religious institutions should fulfil the following broad conditions:

1. It should be under cultivation.
2. It should be under the open sky.
3. It must be suitable for producing sugarcane, wheat and barley.
4. It may have a treasure-trove.
5. It should be free from all obstacles.

In no case should it be (a) saline land (b) a burnt land (c) near the place of cremation and (d) inhabited by wicked people.

This description presents an ideal picture of land gifts but in reality the land grants were made mostly in frontier land where the forest had to be cleared for cultivation and the Brahmanas served the purpose of the development and management of new areas by recruiting tenants and serfs from tribal people and also by their theoretical knowledge of agriculture.[16] Since the view is based on epigraphical testimony it appears more convincing and a practical reason for granting lands to Brahmanas as *dana*. The frontier land was not fertile in nature and required more labour and patience. At least in the initial stage it was not beneficial to the donees. But the tribal people could be absorbed into the Brahmanical social system through the process of acculturation which may be considered an asset to the economy as well.

Land grants made to Brahmanas and religious institutions were in principle perpetual and they contained a request addressed to present and future rulers and officers to see that they were not confiscated or abrogated. The inscriptions generally contain some imprecatory verses pronouncing a curse for those who dared to confiscate such grants. Attention may be drawn to the fact that in the earlier records verses lauding gifts and deprecating their resumption are very few in number but in later records their number increases which may be taken to suggest the growing apprehension of confiscation or resumption of land grants.[17] It appears that with the passage of time kings sometimes resorted to the practice of confiscating or resuming grants of land made to the Brahmanas and religious institutions. That is why in some land charters and law-books great importance has been attached to the honouring of grants made by former kings. The merit accrued from the renewal of land-grants is stated to be equal to the merit accruing from fresh land gifts.[18] Kings have been fully assured that they would be entitled to the same merit whether they make grants by themselves or they honour the grants of land made by their predecessors.[19] It was considered a part of their duty to ensure that grants made by former kings were not abrogated.[20] It is stated that for a ruler it was easy to issue fresh grants of land but most difficult to honour grants made by others; thus it was believed that the honouring of gifts made by others was a more meritorious act than making of gifts. The value of preservation of grants is said to have been higher than that of making gifts afresh.[21] The imprecatory verses generally contain a proclamation that those guilty of confiscating land gifts would certainly go to hell after death.[22] Kings who dared to confiscate land grants made to the Brahmanas and religious institutions would be committing a sin equal to killing a Brahmana.[23] Significantly enough, the Dharmasastra tradition has some provision for the expiation of those found guilty of the murder of a Brahmana[24] but nothing could expiate the sins caused by the resumption of Brahmana lands. The pilgrimage of the holiest place[25], construction of thousands of water reservoirs, performing hundred Asvamedha rites or gift of cows numbering on Koti would not suffice for the expiation of the sin incurred by the confiscation of donated lands.[26] Moreover one, guilty of confiscating even a smallest piece of land will forfeit all other merits attained by the observance of truth and by different kinds of oblation in the fire.[27] Thus, there was unanimity on the issue of honouring gifts of land made by former rulers to Brahmanas. By violating the injunctions, the guilty would lead a miserable life in this world as well as in the next world.

The epigraphic testimony reveals that land grants made to Brahmanas by kings were generally honoured by their successors. The Vakataka ruler Pravarsasena II, the Maitraka King Dharasena, the later Gupta monarch Jivitagupta II, the Maukhari rulers Sarvavarman and Avantivarman and Mahasamanta Maharaja Samudrasena are said to have renewed the grants of land made by their predecessors to Brahmanas and temples.[28] The Deobarnarka inscription[29] of the time of Jivitagupta II informs us that the grant of a village to the sun temple was originally made by the Gutpa ruler Baladitya and subsequently renewed by the Maukharis and the later Guptas, though the Maukharis were the traditional enemies of the later Guptas. But the instances are not lacking when the land grants made by former kings were resumed by their successors. It is stated in the Talamanchi plates of Chalukya Vikramaditya I (dated 660 AD) that he reestablished the endowments of the temples and Brahmanas that had been lost in three kingdoms.[30] In an inscription of Indraraja III dated Saka 836 it is mentioned that the king restored 400 villages that had been confiscated by former kings.[31] The Rajatarangini of Kalhana refers to several cases of confiscation or resumption of land grants. King Vajraditya is said to have resumed a series of different endowments of his father from Parihaspur.[32] King Jayapida is said to have confiscated the property of the Brahmanas[33] and resumed lands of Tulamulya.[34] However, after some time he ceased to confiscate only the *agraharas* but did not release the lands which had been seized by him.[35] Another ruler Sankaravarman is said to have resumed the villages in the possession of the temples by compensation and resorted to direct cultivation.[36] King Harsa of Kashmir confiscated the grants of villages and entire property of the temples.[37]

A pertinent question arises as to why the rulers confiscated or resumed grants of land and villages made to Brahmanas and religious instiutions? It is possible that sometimes kings on account of their religious fanaticism deprived the beneficiaries belonging to other religions. This is revealed by a story in the *Skanda Purana* which relates to Kumarapala who had embraced Jainism and confiscated lands and villages donated to the Brahmanas.[38] It appears that greed, lasciviousness, arrogance or arbitrary will kings may have been partly responsible for deprivation of land and villages donated to the Brahmanas and religious institutions. Vajraditya, Jayapida, Sankaravarman and Harsa were wicked and oppressive rulers of Kashmir who resorted to the practice of amassing wealth by resumption of religious grants. They are said to have persecuted the people, robbed them through the device of various imposts and deprived many people of their life.[39] It may be presumed that the excessive land grants to Brahmanas and religious institutions in the early medieval period must have deprived the state of a considerable income which may have forced some of the rulers to confiscate or resume grants (made by their predecessors) to meet the ever increasing burden of expenditure particularly in an age when warfare had become frequent and the resources of the rulers were dwindling on account of feudal tendencies. This may explain to some extent why the authors of the epigraphical records and law-books attached more importance to the renewal of grants than to the making of land grants afresh. Somadeva Suri in his

Nitivakyamrta (10th CAD) advised the kings to grant a piece of land measuring only a *goruta-pramana* (a distance to which a cow's lowing may be heard) to temples and Brahmanas so that it could be easily maintained by the donors as well as the donees.[40] Vijnanesvara considered the protection of the subjects more valuable than making gifts of land and other things.[41] How far the kings heeded the aforesaid advice, is not known. But the growing practice of alienation of land particularly to the religious beneficiaries was perhaps not considered a wise step by some of the contemporary thinkers.

On the basis of the aforesaid discussion and evidences the following conclusions may be drawn:

1. Land gift was considered the most valuable gift in early India and grants were made to Brahmanas and religious institutions mainly by the ruling class and wealthy people.
2. In principle only fertile land was considered suitable for *dana* but in practice it was seldom observed. Most of the land grants to Brahmanas were made in the frontier land or tribal regions.
3. Confiscation or resumption of the grants of land made to the Brahmanas and religious institutions was considered as the greatest sin but some of the rulers resorted to this practice owing to various socio-religious and socio-economic reasons.
4. Owing to arbitrary will, arrogance, greed and lasciviousness of kings in early medieval India many of the Brahmanas and religious institutions were deprived of land and villages donated to them.

NOTES AND REFERENCES

1. *Manu Smriti*, VII. 84.
2. Ibid., VII. 85.

3. Ibid., IV. 234.
4. Ibid., IV. 230.
5. Ibid., IV. 230.
6. Yaj. I. 210.
7. Ibid., I. 214.
8. *Vasistha Dharmasutra* 29.19; *Brhaspati* 18 cited by P.V. Kane, *History of Dharmasastra* Vol. II, Part II, p. 848.
9. Anusasana Parva 62.2.
10. Quoted by Aparārka, p. 369.
11. Quoted by Aparārka, pp. 289-90.
12. Cf. P.V. Kane, op. cit., p. 869.
13. E.I. II, p. 360; VII, p. 93; VIII. p. 287; 89; XI, pp. 312-13.
14. The Philosophy and Socio-Economic Context of Land Grants in Ancient India, Paper presented to IHC 1980, Section I.
15. *Danakanda of Krtyakalpataru,* ed. K.V. Rangaswami Aiyangar, Vol. V, Baroda 1941, pp. 187-88, 191-93.
16. D.D. Kosambi, *An Introduction to the Study of Indian History,* Bombay, 1956, p. 280; R.S. Sharma, *Indian Feudalism*, Calcutta, 1965, pp. 39-41; D.N. Jha *Proceedings of the Indian History Congress,* 40th Session, 1979 pp. 21 f.
17. Kane has enlisted forty-three such verses pointing out wherever possible their source in the Smritis and in the earliest epigraphs.
18. E.I. II, p. 360; IHQ 1932 Vol. III, p. 305.
19. E.I. XV, p. 5.
20. E.I. IX, p. 37 (Saka 836); E.I. X p. 67 (Saka 815).
21. E.I. VIII, p. 287, *Danadvisistam paripalanam tu.*
22. P.V. Kane, op. cit., p. 1275, fn. 28; p. 1277 fn 39.
23. E.I. XIII, p. 173 (Saka 977).
24. Yaj. III, 250; *Mitakshara* on Yaj. III. 250.
25. E.I. XIII, p. 22, Belgaum Inscription of A.D. 1204.
26. Brhaspati 38; E.I. XIII pp. 280-81; E.I. XI, pp. 282-83; *Padma Purana* VI, 33-38.
27. E.I. XIII, pp. 312-13.
28. Cf. R.P. Tripathi, *Studies in Political and Socio-Economic History of Early India,* Allahabad, 1981, p. 89.
29. Fleet, CII Vol. III, pp. 213 ff.

30. E.I. IX, p. 100.
31. E.I. IX, p. 24. *Purvaprithvipalaviluptani,* p. 33.
32. *Rajatarangini,* Eng. Trans, R.S. Pandit, Allahabad, 1935, IV. 395.
33. Ibid., IV. 632.
34. Ibid., IV. 638.
35. Ibid., IV. 639.
36. Ibid., V. 170.
37. Ibid., VII. 1103-04.
38. *Skanda Purana* 2.3.36.59, 183 cited by B.N.S. Yadava, *Society and Culture in Northern India in the Twelfth Century,* Allahabad, 1973, p. 165.
39. Cf. R.P. Tripathi, op. cit., pp. 90-91.
40. Niti. 19.24 *Devadvijapradeya go-ruta-pramana bhumirdatura-datuscha Sukh-nirvaha.*
41. *Mitakshara* on Yajnavalkya I. 335.

9

Early Indian Thought of Time

A.K. Sinha

The four-yuga theory in ancient Indian traditions is a historical and time-measured notion. It is with such an inseparable relation between the two that the lack of historical consciousness of ancient Indians has been tried to be explained in terms of an unscientific notion of time in ancient India. Theoretically, chronology or the knowledge of the rational sequence of time-measure has been considered as one of the major factors for the so-called historylessness of the ancient Indian people. But, the most important point in this connection which is, unfortunately, overlooked is that both–the time and history require a specific cultural framework within which, not only their notions, but their 'tangets' can also be made clear. The present study proceeds with the first step in this direction by making an attempt to connect and to correlate the traces of the notions and dimensions of time in ancient Indian thought with a view of furthering a study in the nature of Indian culture and its historical consciousness.

There is nothing beyond the span of time.[1] Time, therefore, seems to be primary, if not constituent, cause of the Universe and its very first idea is not beyond the mythological descriptions in any of the world cultures, and

Indian culture is not an exception to it. The Indian counterpart of Time is Kala originated from the word *kal* which bears various meanings[2] although the most dominant sense it indicates is connected with motion. Thus, *Kala* is that which makes things move.[3] In the *Nirukta* of Yaska *Kala* is said to have originated from the root *kalay* which also means motion.[4] In Panini, it is associated, primarily, with motion and change although in its general use the word stands for duration.[5] *Mahabhasya* commenting on Panini, associates *Kala* with motion and hence with change[6] because any motion would necessarily lead to a change. This etymology of the word *Kala* has been the primary basis for all its conceptual developments which finally culminated to consider *Kala* as the supreme power in the Universe causing all changes. As the change is also a state, the other side of this consideration appears to mean that *Kala* was thought to be the root cause for all states, stationary or mobile. The traditional concept of *Kala* seems to be two-dimensional, the eternal or transcendental and the empirical or temporal. The words 'subjective' and 'objective' may also be used for the two dimensions of *Kala*. These two dimensions, though, appear to be opposite to each other, in reality, they are not. Transcendental is not necessarily the negation of the temporal. It is just an advancement of the temporal indicating the progress in journey from finite to infinite, from body to soul. Transcendental or eternal is an all-inclusive reality, in which all temporal realities are submerged. This spirit of Indian culture is best exhibited in the philosophy of *Purusartha Catustaya* which puts before us an example of the synthesis of the two worlds, the transcendental and the temporal. The two-dimensional concept of *Kala* is also to be understood likewise. *Kala* in Indian tradition, is eternal and temporal as well. Temporal, actually, is the manifestation of the eternal and, therefore, *Kala* is the *murti* of the *amurtimana* as the *Maitri Upanisad* declares it to be.[7] It is in and through the *Kala* that the *caya* and *apacaya* (growth and decay) of the *murtis*[8] (objects) take place and can be known. *Kala* is *janyanama janakah*, and therefore, is the first creator from whom everything including the Universe and its objects are originated.[9] It is the first cause of the Universe. Whatever we experience is just a manifestation of it. That is why *Kala,* in Indian tradition, has been equated with *Brahman,* God or Creator who creates, controls and regulates the world and worldly objects and affairs according to his own will.[10] This led the notion of *Kala* into such a direction where *Kala* came to be understood in the sense of *niyati* or fate giving the karman theory a fatalistic face[11] and rejecting altogether the ideas of the freedom of will and action. These are some shades which the Indian concept of *Kala* has undergone.

The word *Kala* in the *Rgveda* appears only once and that too in the sense of proper time[12] but the ideas regarding its eternity and final causality may very clearly be seen in it. In this sense, it has been tried to be equated with *Rta* which has also been considered as the primary cause of all states, mobile and stationary.[13] The best example of this eternity of *Kala* may be seen in the *Purusa Sukta,* wherein *Purusa* is said to have been all that 'has been' and 'will be'. *Purusa* was there before the past and he will be there after the future. Past, present and future are nothing but the partial manifestations of HIM. The sun and the moon, the responsible causes for division of time in day and night, and the order of the seasons at the temporal level have been originated from the different parts of the *Purusa*. When *Purusa* performed sacrifice—the spring was its ghee, the summer was the fuel and the autumn appeared as the oblation.[14] In the *Nasadiya Sukta* of the *Rgveda* it is said that in the beginning there was no division of day and night.[15] But the same text at another place speaks of a wheel rotating in the *Dyau loka* with twelve non-destructible *are* which have been taken to indicate the twelve months of a year.[16] The *Prajapati Sukta* of the *Sukla Yajurveda* speaks of *nimesa,* etc., the division of time, having been created by God.[17] The *Yajurveda* again mentions three hundred and sixty days or seven hundred and twenty days and nights, if taken separately, in a year.[18] *Samvatsara, Parivatsara, Vatsara, Ahoratra, Ardhamasa, Masa* and *Rtu* are the words found frequently in Vedic literature[19] which speaks of the time-consciousness of the people of those days for practical purposes. *Kala* has been discussed in the *Atharvaveda* in great detail, wherein it is described as a horse with seven bridles. It is taken as the Creator and the Sustainer of the Universe. It resembles *Samvatsara*, which is limited and destructible. The seasons, here have been numbered as seven. *Kala* is conceived as uncreated and as such, it is lord of all. It is the creator of self-born *Kasyapa* and tapas. It controls and guides all the gods and the lokas. It is said to be the Creator and Sustainer even of *Dyau, mana* and *prana*, which are all mingled into *kala*.[20]

The *Satapatha Brahmana* writes, "the sacrifice is the equal measure with the year; he offers five libations for sacrifice is commensurate with the year and there are five seasons in a year."[21] The *Aitareya* and *Satapatha Brahman* speak of a year consisting of three hundred and sixty days.[22] The detailed descriptions of the division of time can be seen in *Brahmana* texts, especially the *Aitarea* and the *Satapatha*. Maintaining the calendar was thought to be one of the two purposes which the sacrifices served in the days of the *Brahmanas*.[23] Day and night are conceived as the two wheels of the chariot-like year because on these two the year revolves, thus says the *Aitareya Brahmana*.[24] The *Satapatha Brahmana* establishes an inseparable relation between the day and night and the year when it says that 'one year, in fact, is nothing but days and nights since these two revolving produce it',[25] and at another place it observes that 'the days and nights of the year revolve in an uninterrupted unbroken continuity'.[26] Thus, the empirical or temporal form of *kala* seems to be dominant in the *Brahmanas* while in the age of the *Aranyakas, kala* again, appears in its two-dimensional form. *Taittiriya Aranyaka* mentions empirical *kala* at one place.[27] In the *Aitareya Aranyaka, Prana* is pecullarly indentified with day and night which, at once, is the symbol of time. Day is described as the form of *prana* and night has the form of *apana*. This concept of *Kala* suggests that *Kala* or time, like *prana,* is the ultimate principle.[28] The *Sankhyayana Aranyaka* states that the time unites, procession (*gati*), recession (*nivrtti*) and stasts (*sthiti*) and by this it united the whole Universe.[29] In the Upanisadic days, *Kala* has been considered to be the source of everything in the Universe but, at the same time, the usages of the word *kala* indicating duration or period or division of time, may also be seen very frequently in these texts. The *Chandogya Upanisad* mentions the word *kala* as indicating the 'end' (of something or process).[30] The *Brhdaranyaka Upanisad* uses the word *kala* more than once to mean the 'period' or duration[31] and the *Kausitaki Upanisad* also mentions this word in the same sense.[32] But there are a number of Upanisadic references to show that apart from its empirical or temporal notions *kala* was greatly considered the primary source of the Universe, sometimes inseparable to *Brahmana* and at the other times *Brahman* itself. The *Svetasvatara Upanisad*[33] mentions the word *kala* in the sense of the primary cause of the Universe, whereas the *Mandukya Upanisad* considers the past, present and future as the partial manifestation of *OM*. These three divisions of *kala* are *OM* but *OM* is something more than all this.[34] The *Maitri*

Upanisad discusses the nature of *kala* in great detail. It considers *anna* the source of the whole world and *kala,* the source of *anna.* The sun is considered to be the source of *kala.*[35] It again recognizes *kala* as the supreme power which creates, then maintains and finally destroys the whole world. The same Upanisad identifies *kala* with *Brahman* when it says that the *Brahman* has two forms, *kala* and *Akala,* that which exists before the sun is *akala* and is indivisible but the others originated from the Sun, is *kala* and that is divisible. *Varsa* or year is that part of *kala* which is divisible. All creatures are created by *verva,* sustained by *versa* and in the last are dissolved into *versa.* Therefore, *versa* is the *Prajapati,* the *kala,* the *Brahmaneeda* (shelter of *Brahma*) and is the Self.[36] Thus, *kala* in the Upanisads is both eternal and temporal but the latter has been considered the manifestation of the former and hence inferior to it while the former is equalized with *Brahman,* the primary cause of creation.[37]

In the *Mahabharata*[38] and the *Puranas*[39] it has been dealt with in great detail and the *Smrtis*[40] and other traditional texts are also not unaware of it. The impersonalized *kala* of the earlier days appeared in these texts in a personified *Brahma,* in the names of either the *Kala* himself, or any of the *Brahma, Prajapati, Visnu, Krsna,* etc. An important addition in the concept of the etenal *kala* may be seen in the Epics and the Puranas, which recognize the *kala* as *antaka* meaning one who brings to their end, and then *kala* came to be recognized as the god of death.[41] In these texts too, empirical *kala* has been considered to be the manifestation or creation of the eternal for practical purposes. The idea of this empirical *kala* occupies different shades in the various systems of Indian philosophy including Buddhism and Jainism, which all take it either as a *dravya* (or matter), an image of the subject, a duration or a *vibhu,* a cause or a word only.[42] But they all agree with its empirical or temporal nature which can be known through the changes in the states of an object or phenomenon. Bhartrhari in his *Vakapadiya* describes *kala* as the string puller or *Sutradhara* in the puppet show of the world which brings about an ordered sequence in the world by means of his permissive (*adhyanujna*) and preventive (*pratibandha*) powers. In the absence of the preventive power of time, there would be neither a sequence nor progression nor regression. All actions would be simultaneous and absolute chaos would reign.[43] "The subjective awareness of time brought into sharp relief the contrast of the timelessness of pure consciousness with the temporality of experience and its world. From this contrast the Indian psyche drew its orientation towards the transcendence of time and hence of experience and reality. On the other hand, time was felt to be necessary for action and its consequences. *Karman* matures in time and so does spiritual praxis. The temporal process in which men act, experience and prepare for their transcendental destiny is a cyclic process. Underlying the unchanging cycles of times individual and social is the 'still-point' of eternity."[44] With these interlinking traces between the eternal and temporal notions, the physical or objective time in the form of periods or durations appears with its range from the atomic to the cosmic levels. Although, the traces of these divisions in the names of *Parivatsara, Samvatsara, Idavatsara, Ahoratra* and *masa,* etc. are found since the Vedic days.[45] They are presented with the minutest details in the texts of the later days. *Ksana, lava, nimesa, kastha, kala, muhurta, vama, ahoratra, ardhamasa, masa, rtu, ayana, samvatsara, yuga, kalpa, manavantara, pralaya* and *mahapralaya,* etc., have been mentioned as the units for measuring the time in the later-day texts which also speak of the mutual relationship of these. *Ksana,* in this system of measurement of time stands to be the smallest unit which equalizes 2/45 of a second.[46] Two *ksanas* make one *lava,* two *lavas* make one *nimesa.*[47] Eighteen (or fifteen in some texts) *nimesas* make one *kastha,* thirty *kasthas* equalize one *kala.* Thirty *kalas* with an addition of three *kasthas* make a *muhurta.* Thirty *muhurtas* stand for a day and night and thirty days and nights make a month. Six months make an *ayana* and two *ayanas* or twelve months make one year. Then comes one divine day and night which is equal to one earthly year. Four thousand eighteen hundred divine years make one *Satayuga* which is followed by *Treta, Dwapara* and *Kaliyuga* which are all of three thousand and six hundred, two thousand and four hundred and one thousand and two hundred divine years, respectively. This includes the transitional periods, viz. *Sandhya* and *Sandhyansa* appearing between any of the two *yugas.* Thus twelve thousand divine years make a four-yuga cycle. About seventy-one four-yuga cycles are for one *manavantra* or the period between two *Manus.* Fourteen *manavantras* make one day of *Brahma* which is followed by his night of the same duration. The day of *Brahma* is for creation and night for his sleep, termed as *yoganidra.* With *Brahma's* sleep, the great dissolution comes and it lasts till *Brahma* rises in the morning for the next creation.[48]

The *Arthasastra* presents a partly different scale of time where *ksana* is replaced by *tuta.* Here, five, and not the eighteen, *nimessas* make one *kastha.* Forty *kasthas* make a *nalika* and two *nalikas* make a *muhurta,*[49] Yuga, here, is said to be of five years as in the *Vedangajyotisa,*[50] as Pande says.[51] Astronomy presents a greater refinement in measurement of time. *Suryasiddhanta,* distinguishes time, the destroyer, from time, the calculus, and divides the latter into gross and subtle or concrete and abstract, termed as *murta* and *amurta* respectively, where *murta* is division of time beginning with *prana* and *amurta* began with *truti*.[52] One *prana* or breathing time is equal to ten *vikalpas* and is equated to four seconds. Six *pranas* or sixty *vikalpas* make one *pala* and sixty *palas* make one *nadi* or *ghati* or *danda* which equals twenty-four minutes. *Amurta* time begins with *truti* which is said to be the time taken to pierce a lotus leaf and works out to be 1/3240000 of one second. Sixty *trutis* make one *renu* and sixty *renus* one *lava,* sixty *lavas* one *liksaka* and sixty *liksakas* one *prana* or four seconds.[53] It is to be noted here that the minutest division of time is subjective determination in terms of the rhythm of breathing or working or pronouncing short or long syllables. They were relevant rather to yoga or music. The smaller unit like *truti,* etc. really 'constructive' and arose as fractions relevant in astronomical calculations seeking to avoid cumulative errors. As measures of objective motion they were not actually observational units.[54] Thus from the smallest to the largest units, time has been measured constituting the exterior appearance of the *kala* external. It runs within these divisions but still exists beyond these. *Kala* is all that is and is, also, all that is not.

NOTES AND REFERENCES

1. Broad, C.D., 'Time' in *Encyclopaedia of Religion and Ethics,* Vol. 12, Edinburgh, 1980, pp. 234 f. Also Whitrow, G.J., 'Time' in *The Encyclopaedia Americana* (International Edition), Vol. 26, 1988, pp. 750 f.
2. For various meanings of *kala,* See Apte, V.S., *Sanskrit-English Dictionary,* p. 137; Williams, M., *Sanskrit-English Dictionary,* p. 278.
3. *Kalayati iti Kalah. Kalah Kalayate lokam kalah kalayate jagata, kalah kalayate visvam ten kao bhidhiyate.*
4. *kalah kalayatergatikarmadah, Nirukta,* 2.25.1.
5. *Astadhyayi of Panini,* 3.3.167.
6. *Mahabhasya Vartika on Panini,* 2.2.5.
7. *Kao murtih amurtanama, Maitri Upanisada,* 6.14.

8. *Yen murtinamupacayascapacayasca laksyante ten kalamahuh. Mahabhasya Vartika on Panini,* 2.2.5.
9. Pande, G.C., *An Approach to Indian Culture and Civilization,* Varanasi, 1984, p. 119.
10. This tendency is seen very clearly in the *Atharvaveda* (19.53.6) and since then it continues in the *Aranyakas, Upanisads, Epics* and *Puranas* and the other texts of the later days.
11. cf. Devaraj, N.K., *The Mind and Spirit of India,* Varanasi, 1967, p. 340.
12. *Rgveda,* 10.42.9; Kane, P.V., *History of Dharmasastra* (Hindi tr.), Part 4, Lucknow, 1974, p. 238.
13. cf. Nikam, N.A., *Some Concepts of Indian Culture,* Shimla, 1973, pp. 2-3. See, also, Zimmerman, R., The Evidence of Rk-Texts for the Meaning of Rta in the *Proceedings of All India Oriental Conference,* 5th session, Vol. 1, Lahore, 1930, pp. 214, 217.
14. *Rgveda,* 10.90.2.6, 13-14.
15. Ibid., 10.129.2.
16. Ibid., 1.164.2. For details, see, Mandal, K.K., *A Comparative Study of the Concepts of Time and Space in Ancient India,* Varanasi, 1968, Ch. 1.
17. *Yajurveda,* 21.1.5.2.
18. Ibid., 27.45.
19. For details of these divisions, see, Kane, P.V., op. cit., p. 247; Mandal, K.K., op. cit., Ch. 1.
20. *Atharvaveda,* 19.53.1, 4,6,7,8,10; 54.1, 4, 5.
21. *Satapatha Brahmana* 3.1.3.17; Basu, J., *India in the Age of the Brahmanas,* Calcutta, 1969, p. 261.
22. *Aitareya Brahmana* 2.7.7: *Satapatha Brahmana* 1.3.5.9.
23. Basu, J., op. cit., p. 262.
24. *Ete Ha Vai Samvatsarasya Cakre yadahoratre tabhyameya tatsamvatsarameti, Aitareya Brahmana,* 5.25.5.
25. *Satapatha Brahmana* 3.2.2.4.
26. Ibid., 1.3.5.16.
27. *Taittiriya Aranyaka,* 1.2.1.
28. Mandal, K.K., op. cit., Ch. 2.
29. *Sankhyayana Aranyaka,* 7, quoted by Pathak, V.S., *Ancient Historians of India* (2nd edn.), Gorakhpur, 1984, p. 28.

30. *Chandogya Upanisada,* 2.31.1.
31. *Bradharanyaka Upanisada,* 1.2.4.
32. *Kausitaki Upanisada,* 1.2.5.
33. *Svetasvatara Upanisada,* 1.1-2.
34. *bhutam bhavad bhavisyamiti sarvemomkar eva. Yaccanyat trikalatitam tadapyomkara eva, Mandukya Upanisada,* 1.
35. *Maitri Upanisasa,* 6.14.
36. Ibid., 6.15-16.
37. *Svetasvatara Upanisada,* 6.1-5.
38. *Mahabharata,* 1.1.248-250, 227.35, 41, 56, 83, 83-85, 92-97; 231, 11-17, 20, 21, 29, 30; 234.5, 19, 25, 39, 45, 51-52; 238, 19-20.
39. *Visnu Purana,* 2.14, 15, 17-19; 15.22, 38, 55-57; *Vayu Purana,* 32.29-30; *Kurma Purana,* 2.2.16; *Bhagvata Purana,* 3.11.3-7; *Visnudharmottara Purana,* 1.72, 1-7.
40. *Manusmrti,* 1.21.24.
41. cf. *Mahabharata (Striparva),* 2.24, *Vayu Purana,* 32, 29-30.
42. Kane, P.V., op. cit., pp. 241-242; Pande, G.C., op. cit., p. 119.
43. *Vakyapadiya,* 3.9.4.5; Pathak, V.S., op. cit., p. 28.
44. Pande, G.C., op. cit., p. 120.
45. *Rgveda,* 1.110.4; 1.140.2; 10.62.2; *Taittiriya Samhita,* 5.5.7.1-3; *Vajasaneyi Samhita,* 27.45; *Atharvaveda,* 6.55.2; *Taittiriya Brahamana,* 1.4.10.1; *Brhadaranyaka Upanisada,* 3.8.9.
46. Seal, B.N., *The Positive Sciences of the Ancient Hindus,* p. 77, vide, Pande, G.C., op. cit., p. 120.
47. *Ksana-dvayam lavah prokto nimesastu lavadvayama, Kiranavali,* quoted by Seal, B.N., op. cit., p. 77.
48. *Mahabharata,* 12.231.12-30; *Manusmrti,* 1.64; *Visnu Purana* 3.8.22; also *Brahmanda Purana,* 231.64.12; *Kurma Purana,* 5.3.4-20.
49. *Arthasastra* (ed.) R.P. Kangle, Vol. 1, Bombay, 1962, 2.20.29-36.
50. *Pancasamvatsaro yugamiti,* Ibid., 2.20.64.
51. Pande, G.C., op. cit., p. 120.
52. *Surya Siddhanta,* 1.10; Kane, P.V., op. cit., p. 242.
53. *Surya Siddhanta,* p. 7; quoted by Pande, G.C., op. cit., p. 121, 133 fn.
54. Pande, G.C., op. cit., p. 121.

10

Acheulian Culture in the Middle Son Valley

J.N. Pal

Introduction

As a result of archaeological researches in the Vindhyan region in north-central India during the last five decades the reconstruction of developmental phases of prehistoric cultures has been made. Son river valley has emerged archaeologically as one of the significant regions of the Vindhyas. It preserves extensive alluvial deposits that accumulated during the Middle and Upper Pleistocene periods. Artefacts from Lower Palaeolithic to Mesolithic have been found in situ in the geological context. Several archaeologists, geologists, geomorphologists and other scientists have taken a keen interest in the study of the region. Archaeological investigations have been done in the middle Son valley (parts of district Sonbhadra in Uttar Pradesh and that of Sidhi in Madhya Pradesh, bounded by river Kanhar in east, Banas in the west, Kaimur in the north and river Mayar, a tributary of the Rihand, in the south) during the last five decades. A complete prehistoric sequence, with the evidence of transformational stages from one culture to the other, has been brought to light. The palaeo-environment of the region has been reconstructed from geological research and studies of fossil faunal remains. A multi-disciplinary team of archaeologists, under the direction of the present author from University of Allahabad and Dr. Mickel Petraglia from the University of Oxford, carried investigations in the middle Son valley in 2009. This paper presents a brief account of the Acheulian culture in the middle Son River Valley.

The first systematic geo-archaeological investigations were carried in the middle Son valley in 1974-75 by the Department of Ancient History, Culture and Archaeology, University of Allahabad in collaboration with the Geological Survey of India (IAR 1974-75). An extensive area from Baghor in the east to Chorhat in the west covering a distance of 70 kms bounded by Kaimur in the north and Son in the south was explored. A multidisciplinary team from the University of Allahabad and University of California in 1980 under the supervision of Prof. G.R. Sharma and Prof. J. Desmond Clark (Sharma and Clark 1983) conducted extensive investigations in the area. The Middle Son River Valley preserves extensive alluvial deposits, measuring about 30 m in thickness that accumulated during the Middle and Upper Pleistocene periods (Figure 1).

Geological Formations

The geological formations of the Middle River Son Valley are separable into four alluvial and three loess units (Williams and Royce 1982, 1983). The formations from bottom to top are: (1) the Sihawal, (2) Patpara, (3) Baghor and (4) Khetaunhi (Fig. 2). Martin Williams and his team (Williams et al., 2006) subsequently identified an additional formation named Khuteli formation having Toba ash deposits in it. This formation has been placed between Sihawal and Patpara formations. The geological formations of the middle Son valley are as under:

1. Sihawal Formation: The formation is represented at the type site on the left bank of the Son River 1 km east of Sihawal village. It is divisible into two sub-units: (a) Sihawal Formation gravels and (b) Sihawal Formation silt. Combined maximum observed thickness ranges from 1.5 to 4 m. Acheulian artefacts including handaxes, cleavers and flakes have been found mostly from Sihawal Formation gravels and a few from Sihawal Formation silt as is evident from excavation at Sihawal II (Kenoyer and Pal 1983).

2. Khuteli Formation: The formation, containing volcanic ash, on the right bank of the Son near Khuteli village was named Khuteli Formation. Its cultural relation is still under investigation.

3. Patpara Formation: The type section of Patpara is at the excavated archaeological site of Patpara (Figure 4). With a maximum thickness of 10 m it unconformably overlies on the Sihawal Formation. It is a formation of gravels, clays and fluviatile sands. Refined handaxes, cleavers, prepared cores and flakes are the main artefacts from this formation.

4. Baghor Formation: With a maximum thickness of 20 m the Baghor Formation unconformtably rests on the Patpara Formation. It has two distinct units: (a) coarse member and (b) fine member. Rolled and abraded Middle Palaeolithic along with fresh unabraded Upper Palaeolithic artefacts and a sizeable number of animal fossils were found from the coarse member and fresh Upper Palaeolithic, microlithic blade artefacts from the fine member.

5. Khetaunhi Formation: Forming aggredational terrace approximately 10 m above the present river, it is a 10 m thick deposit of inter-bedded silts and clays with occasional traces of fine sand. Neolithic artefacts including hand made pottery, microlithic bladelets and celts are the archaeological material from the formation.

Palaeolithic Cultures and Palaeo Environment

Research in the past 50 years in the area had resulted in an accurate reconstruction of Palaeolithic occupation (Sharma 1980; Sharma and Clark 1983; Clark and Williams 1987, 1990; Williams and Royce 1982; Williams and Clarke 1984, 1995; Jones and Pal 2005; Pal et al., 2005; Williams et al., 2006; Haslam et al., 1911). The geological formations have presented a vertical record of the climatic changes through which the Son has undergone from mid Pleistocene to early Holocene periods. During the accumulation of Sihawal Formation climate ranged from semi-arid to sub-humid. The basal gravel of Sihawal Formation represents a high energy fluviatile bed load deposit in semi-arid climate with intermittent and erratic rainfall and sparse to absent plant cover. The silt resting on it represents relatively dry climate, semi-arid to sub-humid, which was deposited by low energy streams unable to carry coarser material. The Patpara Formation appears to have come into existence under high flow water regime. Widespread leaching and precipitation of iron and manganese implies sub-humid conditions during and after the initial phases of widespread valley aggredation. The Baghor Formation with its lower and upper members indicate a change from bed-load to suspended load regime which are tentatively attributed to the cold, dry terminal Pleistocene and warm and wet early Holocene respectively. The youngest, Khetaunhi Formation, indicates a return to sub-humid conditions following an interval of hill slope instability and river incision.

Lower Palaeolithic (Acheulian) artefacts have been found from the Sihawal Formation while Lower and Middle Palaeolithic artefacts have been recovered from the Patpara Formation. The coarse member of Baghor Formation has yielded fresh Upper Palaeolithic artefacts and rolled middle

Palaeolithic artefacts. The upper unit of the formation yielded late Upper Palaeolithic and early Mesolithic artefacts. The Khetaunhi formation contained microliths and Neolithic artefacts. The Neolithic habitation site of Kunjhun, on the right bank of the river, is on top of this terrace formation.

Major fieldwork in the valley by a multi-disciplinary team was done in 1980 and 1982 (Sharma 1980; Sharma and Clark 1983; Clark and Williams 1987, 1990; Williams and Royce 1982; Williams and Clarke 1984, 1995). Some minor fieldwork to collect samples for dating and other studies has been done (Pal et al., 2005, Jones and Pal 2005, Williams et al., 2006) and several absolute dates, confined to the Upper Pleistocene and Holocene periods, have been determined using a range of chronometric techniques and have provided chronology for various sedimentary contexts within these formations (Mandal 1983; Williams and Clarke 1984, 1995; Pal et al., 2005; Williams et al., 2006). Thus now we have some dates for almost all the formations, though these are still tentative and need more authentic dates for confirmation.

The artefacts recovered from different geological deposits and excavated and explored primary/semi-primary context sites belonging to different phases of Palaeolithic cultures show a remarkable technotypological evolution. The Lower Palaeolithic assemblage includes handaxes (including lanceolate and picks), cleavers, scrapers, knives, spheroids, sub-spheroids, etc. along with cores and flakes (Misra 1997). The artefacts are manufactured on quartzite, sand stone, limestone and chert. The Middle Palaeolithic assemblage consists of refined handaxes, discoids, sub-spheroids, scrapers, points, borers, and blades along with cores and flakes. The artefacts are manufactured on limestone, chert, quartzite, flint and jasper. The Upper Palaeolithic assemblage consists of various types of blade tools, burins, borers, scrapers, lunates, etc. The artefacts are made mainly on chert but other silicious stones like chalcedony, jasper, agate are also used. At least three stages have been marked within the Upper Palaeolithic period of the region (Varma and Pal 1997). Stratigraphical evidence shows that the Upper Palaeolithic industries in the region are preceded by the Middle Palaeolithic and succeeded by the Mesolithic.

The explorations in the mid Son valley covering parts of Sidhi district in Madhya Pradesh and parts of Mirzapur district in Uttar Pradesh have resulted in the discovery of 47 Lower Palaeolithic sites- 45 sites in Sidhi and 2 in Mirzapur. Of these as many as 10 sites are factory sites, the important ones being Sihawal, Rampur, Nakjhar, Barbasa-Ki-Pahari, Patpara, Barri, Pandari, Dhup Khari and Hatawa Khari. The location of the factory sites of the Son valley is somewhat different from those of the Belan valley. The Lower Palaeolithic factory sites of the Son valley are situated either on the medial ridge almost running parallel to the Son in the north and dividing the Son valley into two parts or near the bank of the river itself. Among the former group of sites, mention may be made of Patpara, Hatwa, etc., the latter group is represented by Sihawal, Rampur, Nakjhar, Kunjhun, etc. The Lower Palaeolithic assemblage of the Son valley contains handaxes, cleavers, scrapers, knives, spheroids and sub-spheroids, etc. along with cores, flake and debitage. The artifacts are fashioned mainly on quartzite and chert. In the total assemblage there are only two handaxes which are made of quartz. The lithic industry of the Son valley is characterized by high workmanship. Lanceolates and picks constitute a salient feature of the assemblage. The tools generally are marked by shallow flake scars, thin sections and complete removal of the cortex. In the overwhelming majority of the cases, the use of cylinder hammer is suggested. Most of the tools have been fashioned on flakes, preferably on end-flakes.

The Lower Palaeolithic industry of the Son valley compares and contrasts with its counterpart of the Belan valley. The lithic assemblages of both the valleys are characterized by handaxes, cleavers and scrapers. In the majority of cases, tools have been fashioned on quartzite. However, a closer scrutiny of the lithic assemblage of the two river valleys reveals some advanced technological traits in the Son assemblage. In the Son valley, the pebble tools are conspicuous by their absence while in the Belan assemblage these constitute a sizeable number. Lanceolates and picks the evolved shapes in the Lower Palaeolithic assemblage, are well represented in the Son valley, while in that of the Belan these have not been encountered so far. The Belan lithic assemblage is cleaver-dominated but that of the Son valley is dominated by handaxes. Besides, the Belan assemblage as indicated above is characterized by thin section and shallow flake-scars. The tools of the Son valley are reduced in length, width and thickness in comparison to their counterparts of the Belan valley, as would be evident from a comparative study of Tables 2 and 4. The evidence, as it stands, indicates that the Lower Palaeolithic industry of the Son valley represents a late phase compared to that of the Belan.

Manigara in the Adwa valley in Mirzapur district (Pal 2005), Sihawal II (Kenoyer and Pal 1983), Nakjhar Khurd (Misra et al., 1983), Bamburi and Patpara I (Haslam et al., 2011) in the Son valley in Sidhi district and Maihar I (Pandey and Pal 1988) in the Lilji valley in Satna district are the excavated sites of the Lower Palaeolithic culture in the region.

The OSL dates obtained from excavated sites, viz. Patpara and Bamburi suggest that the Acheulian culture in the area survived in 140 ka which has been termed as the youngest Achulian culture (Petraglia et al., 2012).

Figure 1. Locations of Archaeological Sites in the Middle Son Valley

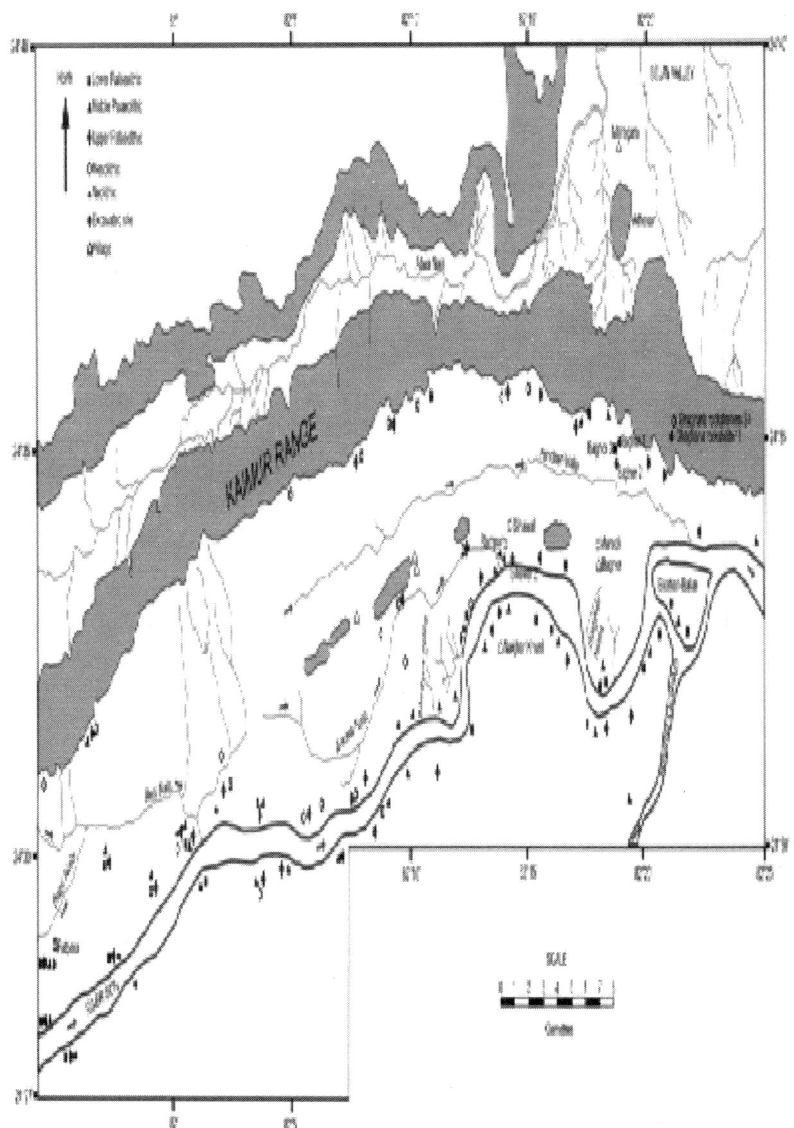

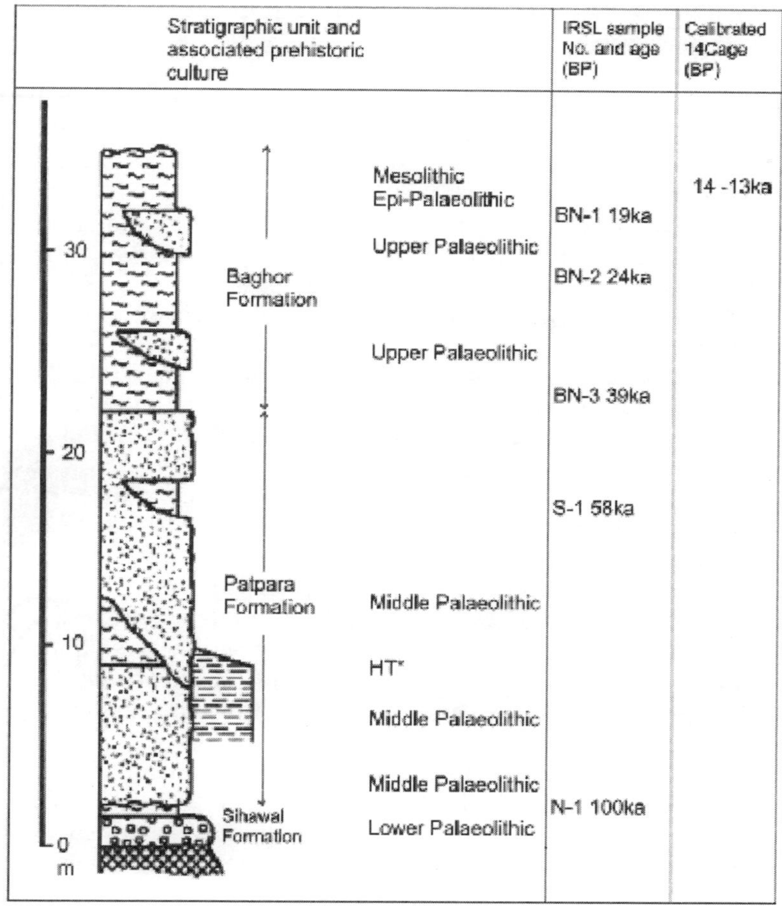

REFERENCES

Clark, J.D. and M.A.J. Williams, 1987. Paleo Environments and Prehistory in North Central India: A Preliminary report. In: Jacobsen, J. (ed.), *Studies in the Archaeology of India and Pakistan.* Aris and Phillips Ltd, Warminster, pp. 19-41.

Clark, J.D. and M.A.J. Williams, 1990. Prehistoric Ecology, Resource Strategies and Culture Change in the Son Valley, Northern Madhya Pradesh, Central India. *Man and Environment* 15, 13-24.

Haslam, M., R.G. Roberts, C. Shipton, J.N. Pal, J. Fenwick, P. Ditchfield, N. Boivin, A.K. Dubey, M.C. Gupta and M. Petraglia,

2011. Late Acheulian Hominins at the Marine Isotope Stage 6/5e Transitionin North-Central India, *Quaternary Research* 75: 670-682.

Jones, C. Sacha and J.N. Pal, 2009. The Palaeolithic of the Middle Son Valley, North-Central India: Changes in Hominin Lithic Technology and Behaviour during the Upper Pleistocene. *Journal of Anthropological Archaeology* 28(3): 323-341.

Kenoyer, J.M. and J.N. Pal, 1983. Report on the Excavation and Analysis of an Upper Acheulian Assemblage from Sihawal II, in *Palaeo-Environment and Prehistory in the Middle Son Valley* (eds. G.R. Sharma and J.D. Clark), Abinash Prakashan, Allahabad, pp. 23-28.

Mandal, D., 1983. A Note on the Radiocarbon Dates from the Middle Son Valley. In: Sharma, G.R. and Clark, J.D. (eds.), *Palaeo-environments and Prehistory in the Middle Son Valley*. Abinash Prakashan, Allahabad, pp. 285-289.

Misra, V.D., 1997. Lower and Middle Palaeolithic Cultures of Northern Vindhyas, in *Indian Prehistory* (eds. V.D. Misra and J.N Pal), Department of Ancient History, Culture and Archaeology, University of Allahabad, Allahabad, pp. 61-74.

Misra, V.D., R.S. Rana, J.D. Clark and R.J. Blumenschine, 1983. Preliminary Excavations at the Son River Setion at Nakjhar Khurd in *Palaeo-Environment and Prehistory in the Middle Son Valley* (eds. G.R. Sharma and J.D. Clark), Abinash Prakashan, Allahabad, pp. 101-115.

Pal, J.N., 2005. A History of the Development of Human Cultures in the Tons Valley, in K.K. Chakravarty and G.L. Badam (eds.) *River Valley Cultures of India*, Indira Gandhi Rashtriya Manav Sangrahalaya, Bhopal and Aryan Books International, New Delhi, pp. 45-57.

Pal, J.N., M.A.J. Williams, M. Jayaswal and A.K. Singhvi, 2005, Infra Red Stimulated Luminescence Ages for Prehistoric Cultures in the Son and Belan Valleys, North Central India, *Journal of Interdisciplinary Studies in History and Archaeology*, Volume 1, Number 2 (Winter 2004), pp. 51-62.

Pandey, J.N. and J.N. Pal, 1988 Acheulian Occupation at Maihar, *Man and Environment* XII: 201-202.

Petraglia, M.D., Peter Ditchfield, Sacha Jones, Ravi Korisettar and J.N. Pal 2012. The Toba Volcanic Supereruption Environmental Change, and Hominin Occupation History in India Over the Last 140,000 Years, *Quaternary International* 258: 119-134.

11

Recent Historical Writings: Non-Fiction History vis-à-vis Academic History

Abhay Kumar Singh

A human being, by virtue of his impressionable memory, reflective capacity and reasoning capability, has the right to form opinions about the life around and also express his mind. Whether aware or not, every person is a subject of history; whether a major player or not, but surely a persona of the drama of his times. At the same time, he is the source of the history of his times; and also a demi-historian of some historical episode—if only he has left his mark and his testimony. What matters is that where and how he has testified. While the vigilant and discreet people remained conscious of this fact, and left their progeny behind them, as also their memorials, memoirs, stone-tablets, epigraphs, copper plates and coins; the laymen cared not for this practice due to their *own* realization of their *own* insignificance and neglibgible importance in their contemporary life situation. But despite their low esteem no one can deny the right of forming opinions. And expressing these opinions in one's own interpreted versions could qualitatively vary in degrees: from quasi-history to gossip; from legend to drama; from reflections to conjectures. Notwithstanding the right to opinion, such a version is at best a 'subjective narration', unless proved otherwise: it is comparable to the home-cure recipe rather than a specialist's prescription; an 'unpasteurized concoction' rather than a 'proprietary product'. Yet, it possesses content, observation, elements of true data and chronology, all the ingredients upon which any specialist 'historian' relies for his work.

A silent revolution that occurred in the field of "Non-fiction/History" writing in 2006 was the publication of *The Last Mughal: The Fall of a Dynasty, Delhi, 1857*, by William Dalrymple. The book has been a tremendous success, a bestseller, which has been widely read, admired and awarded. The compliments and appreciation of the critics of calibre, reviewers of stature and readers of significance place the author on the pedestal of a star historian and the book as a landmark historical treatise. Of not less than 53 reviews quoted in the edition, and hundreds of congratulatory notes on websites, we refer here to only those relevant for the theme of our enquiry, i.e., 'Non-Fiction History *vis-a vis* Academic History.'

The Silent Revolution Ushers a 'Think-Aloud' Debate

Many learned opinions consider the book as a treatise of History. It is David Robinson (*The Scotsman, Book of the Year*) who identifies *The Last Mughal* as "the oriental version" of Gibbon's *The Decline and Fall of the Roman Empire*, the renowned book of history. Professor C.M. Naim, who accepts *The Last Mughal* as a "well-reasoned history at its enjoyable best", also gave the reasons that made it outstanding. That, it is "meticulously researched"; that it followed "exemplary fairness and empathy in judgements" on events and people and in selection of episodes; and that it has shown great attention to "literary style".

Others compliment Dalrymple's book as a class of history: "vivid and ambitious revisionist history" (Alex Stewart, *Traveller*) and "remarkably humane and egalitarian history" (David Arnold, *Times Literary Supplement*).

Historians' non-commital comments

The Indian historians have admired the book and recommended its reading, too. Noted historians like Professor Harbans Mukhia (whose assistance is acknowledged by the author) finds it "the most definite account of the events centred on Bahadur Shah Zafar and the great Indian Mutiny in and around Delhi in 1857-58. Based upon an immense amount of empirical research.... Dalrymple achieves an admirable balance between fairness and a moving empathy with the subject of his book."

Professor Mushirul Hasan (*Indian Express*) acknowledges that Dalrymple has "established credentials as a powerful writer" and his is a "painstakingly researched book with plenty of new insights." Professor Nayanjot Lahiri's comment (in the *Hindustan Times*) that the "vivid account of the 1857 resistance" is "different and delightful", suggests that she considers the book as a non-fiction literary historical work: a "vivid and tactile retelling of the story" where "the untidiness of the unfolding drama... makes it extraordinarily human."

Reading between the lines of the above opinions, one is left in doubt if the historians would consider Dalrymple's researched book as a history of 1857 or only a retold story.

Is it a Discourse of History?

Notwithstanding the beauty of the research and style of the book, one may ask if it should be treated as a dissertation on the history of the 1857 uprising, for the purposes of the academics. The answer cannot be "no" nor "yes", unless the finer points are explored. Just for not been written by an academic faculty, the book cannot be denied its placement among a class of academic works; but at the same time the treatment of the source material and the objective of the work, its approach and hypothesis all need to be considered for deciding the nature of even the highest quality of historical writings. There have been different classes of superb historical writings, in fact, biographies, memoirs, historical drama, historical movies, but they are classed as artistic masterpieces and *not* historical treatises. We may say so for the vernacular writings on historical characters and events like *Ananda Math, Aankhon Dekha Ghadar, Jhansi Ki Rani,* or the English *Freedom at Midnight, The Untold Story*, and the books written about the 1975 Emergency. Yet we must acknowledge that *The Last Mughal* is definitely different from all these, because it is researched, referenced and annotated, like an academic work of a versatile historian. If Dalrymple does not possess the credentials of a history teacher, he definitely has the potential to be a perfect one. In fact, a noted expert on Historiography, Professor Bhupendra Yadav, ungrudgingly accepts Dalrymple as a historian due to the merit of his archival research work.

A Work of Real Worth: Its Strength is Research

P.C. Alexander (*The Asian Age*) declares William Dalrymple as "one of the greatest historical writers of our time". What are the merits and strengths of William Dalrymple's work? Bhupesh Bhandari (*Business Standard*) asserts: "William Dalrymple tells things as they happened." As David Washbrook (*Biblio*) maintains Dalrymple's account is a contribution to "academic, as well as...'popular' history." Two opinions emerge about its merits: firstly, the content derived from hitherto unconsulted archival material; and secondly, the style of presentation. Aptly Aamer Hussein (*The Independent*) declares: "Diligently researched and densely informative". Suresh Menon (*Deccan Herald*) noted that Dalrymple's masterpiece "has form ... as fascinating as the content"; it gives a wide-angle sweep from king to layman, and scores on two fronts, "original research and fresh insights". Sara Wheeler (*The Daily Telegraph*) sees the strength in "the breadth of its quotation from unpublished primary sources... In deploying his material, Dalrymple shows he has the two essential gifts of the historian: a grasp of detail, and an ability to see the big picture." Pavan Varma (*DNA*) believes it is the author's "ability to write history in the most gripping manner."

Coup in Researching: The Plus Point

Dalrymple's "coup in researching was his uncovering some 20,000 personal Persian and Urdu papers written by Delhi residents who survived the uprising", notes Tobin Harshaw (*New York Times Book Review*). David Gilmour (*The Spectator*) appreciates, saying, "William Dalrymple recognized the historical value of the 'Mutiny Papers' stacked and ignored on the shelves of the National Archives of India and worked his way through thousands of documents in Persian and Urdu."

Michael Binyon (*The Times*) also credits the sources for the value of the work. He writes: "Dalrymple's towering achievement in providing almost hourly detail lies in his sources. Drawing widely on Persian and Urdu manuscripts, he narrates the chaos through the memoirs, letters, official reports and a sweeping understanding of Indian and Muslim cultures."

Professor Michael H. Fisher notes: "Dalrymple's extensive archival research has enabled him to present a striking new perspective on the tragic events of 1857 as centred in Delhi." Rudrangshu Mukherjee observes that the book is "a poignant story, extremely well narrated, with new facts and analysis."

In the Introduction, William Dalrymple has also wondered about the neglect of the unnoticed sources by the historians at least beyond 1921, since when the Mutiny papers were catalogued in Calcutta and stored and thereafter easily available, "all neatly bound in string and boxed up in the cool, hushed, air-conditioned vaults of the Indian National Archives." (p. 12). He asks, "When ten thousand dissertations and whole shelves of *Subaltern Studies* have carefully and ingeniously theorized about orientalism and colonialism and the imagining of the Other.... not one PhD has ever been written from the Mutiny Papers, no major study has ever systematically explored its contents." He adds, "Yet the collection could not have been in a better-known or more accessible archive—the National Archives of India....in the centre of India's capital city." (p. 14).

On the contrary, despite admitting Dalrymple's thorough archival research, Indian historians have not explained why there was no consultation of that material before by any Indian colleague. It falls in line with our present ways that no scholar feels the accountability to explain to anyone (except the supervisor/examiner) why he ignored or why he paid more heed to any source material. Most of us freely choose our facts like "fish on the fish-monger's slab." If we cannot answer, we must think, at least.

Indian neglect for the antiquities and sources of history has been a sad story for hundreds of years. Al-Beruni had noticed and commented on this tendency. This fact had denied the Indian historians to write their own history first, and let some others take the lead. The re-discovery of Indian history began by the pioneers in the Royal Asiatic Society in 18th century Bengal has not yet ended, and the present archival treasure is also revealed by a zealous adventurer from Europe! Dalrymple (p. 14) shares his delight as a researcher: "Using the Mutiny Papers and properly harvesting their riches as a source for 1857 felt at times strange and exciting—and indeed as unlikely—as going to Paris and discovering, unused on shelves of the Bibliotheque Nationale, the entire records of the French Revolution."

Why has it been so? Possibly, Dalrymple suggests, because the Persian *shikista* script in which the Mutiny papers are generally written is not readable by many. Alas! This extinction in India is a matter to lament: sadly, the knowledge of Persian and its script, an integral part of our national heritage has almost vanished. Where will our research head towards? Is our task limited to give interpretations and narratives or should we not only protect the sources but also the key to decipher those historical sources? What is the responsibility of the Indian historians of the period under reference?

Now, This is History to Learn From

Some comments of certain book-reviewers have in asides or even openly placed questions on the historical writings by historians-by-profession. But they relate more to historiographical aspects—the writing style or diction of history—rather about the content and the careful consultation or neglect of the sources. Jairam Ramesh laments/wishes, "If only other Indian historians—both in India and abroad—emulated him (=*William Dalrymple*)." In the view of David Washbrook (*Biblio*), Dalrymple "rescues 1857 from the hands of imperial apologists and nationalist hagiographers alike. *The Last Mughal* is a major contribution to academic, as well as to so-called 'popular', history." David Robinson (*The Scotsman*) points out that "here history is almost novelistic in its vividness, wonderfully embodying both the closeness to, and radical distance from the past."

To me, the above undefined distinction rests on a functional basis. The "academic history", "popular history" and "novelistic" appear to me to correspond to the better understood categories of "history", "journalistic history" and "historical writings".

The Return of the Historical Narrative

However, Professor Bhupendra Yadav, who is an expert on historiography and author of the commendable work, *Framing History—Context and Perspective,* enlightened me about the ongoing debate between side-takers of 'popular history' and 'academic history', since Lawrence Stone published *The Revival of Narrative,* in 1979. Historians are divided into two camps; the 'structural' and the 'narrative', and the two differ (i) in the choice of what they consider significant in the past, and (ii) their preferred modes of historical explanations. Narrative historians emphasize individual character and intention, while the structural historians prefer explantions which takes the form. Since the 1980s, there has been a shift from analytical to the descriptive mode of historical writing. The distrust with the structural historical explanations, often criticized as "reductionist" or "determinist", has consequently revived the narrative. In 1989 Simon Schama wrote about the French Revolution in a book, *Citizens,* in the form of chronicles where micro-histories were inserted into the major history, and the author preferring to explain the Revolution in terms of decisions taken by individuals, and rejecting to consider it in terms of the structure of institutions.

Prof. Bhupendra Yadav sent me an essay by Peter Burke, entitled "History of Events and the Revival of Narratives". Burke expresses the problem, "If popular history remained faithful to the narrative tradition, academic history became increasingly concerned with problems and with structures." Burke noted that narrative is making a comeback because the structuralists discuss events not for their own sake but for what they reveal about the culture in which they took place. John Millar, Lucien Febvre and Fernand Braudel regarded events as "the surface of the ocean of history, significant only for what they might reveal of the deeper currents." Supporters of narrative say that "analysis of structures is static and in a sense unhistorical."

Interestingly, Burke (p. 287) compares two works on Indian history, viz. Chrisopher Hibbert's *The Great Mutiny* (London 1978) and Eric Stokes' *The Peasant and the Raj* (Cambridge 1978) as two examples of historical writings. Hibbert produced a traditional narrative, "set-piece history in a grand manner" with chapters like 'Mutiny at Meerut', 'The Seige of Lucknow', etc., but it does not tell the reader why the Mutiny occurred. Stokes, however, offered a careful analysis of the geography and sociology of the revolt, its regional variations and its local contexts, yet "drew back from a final synthesis". Burke, then predicted a "potential third book, which might integrate narrative and analysis and relate events more closely to the structural changes in the society." *The Last Mughal*, actualizes Burke's prediction to a great extent.

What Should History Be Like?

Elsewhere, David Robinson remarks, "Dalrymple writes with a brio rare among academic historians." Any "*academic historian*" may ask the intellectual world of non-historians,

"All right, then, what should history be like to suit your expectations?" David Robinson may appreciate a history "almost novelistic in its vividness." S. Prasannarajan (*India Today*) may explain that he praises the book *The Last Mughal*, because here "History ceases to be a dead abstraction... [but] an enduring enchantment." Jairam Ramesh, (*The Hindu, Book of the Year*) who finds it as "history at its archival yet lucid best, might suggest that history should be "both educative and evocative, both enlightening and entertaining." Khushwant Singh (*Outlook*) recommended that *The Last Mughal...* "shows the way history should be written: not as a catalogue of dry-as-dust kings, battles and treaties, but to bring the past to the present; put life back in characters long dead and gone and make the reader feel he is living among them, sharing their joys, sorrows and apprehensions." Mukund Padmanabhan's (*The Hindu*) answer is hidden in the review, "Few writers understand as well as Dalrymple that the function of history in not merely to inform but also to engage and entertain."

Is it a Function of History to "Entertain"?

The object/function of history being "to inform/educate/enlighten" is acceptable, but "to enchant/entertain" is debatable. Narratives are surely enchanting, but it has been said that "narrative is no more innocent in historical wtiting than it is in fiction." History is expected to give us the truth of the past. It is supposed to view the events from all sides so that the facets of the truth should be revealed. The approach requires "analysing" the episodes of history in order to ascertain the forces and factors, as not merely the actors in historical episodes. All this exercise needs to be done with the authentic sources that too have been substantiated and assessed. Thus written, history could be "engaging" yet also be "entertaining" to the wisdom of a scholar. Intellectual entertainment by well reasoned writing is expected, but to guarantee a novel like reading is not always possible.

Going to Peter Burke, again, we learn (p. 289) what should be avoided in writing history: (i) Invention of someone's stream of consciousness; and (ii) the scrambling of temporal sequence. Burke writes, "It might be possible to make civil wars and other conflicts more intelligible by following the model of the novelists who tell their stories from more than one view point.... "Such a device would allow an interpretation of conflict in terms of a conflict of interpretations. To allow the 'varied and opposing voices' of the dead to be heard again; the historian needs, like a novelist, to practise heteroglossia." Further, Burke recommends the historian to let his opinion be 'just one voice', and let him refuse to tell what his story really meant. "More historians are coming to realize that their work does not reproduce 'what actually happened' so much as represent it from a particular point of view. To communicate this awareness to the readers of history, traditional form of narrative is inadequate." (p. 290). However, the modern narrative is equally risky, as temporal continuity is often dismantled in it. Burke feels that "the point of looking for new literary forms is surely the awareness that the old forms are inadequate for one's purposes."

Often the sources of history are scarce, dubious and dull; and the reconstruction of the past has to be dry and catalogue like, to remain fair to the subject. Debates and doubts have to be admitted because uncertainties and controversies invite research to unravel the truth. It is true that style of writing, good language and narration covers up the dreary and dullness of the work. Golo Mann advised that a historian needs "to try to do two different things simultaneously"; "to swim with the stream of events" and "to analyse these events from the position of a later, better informed observer"; combining the two methods "so as to yield a semblance of homogeneity without the narrative falling apart." Interesting histories have been wonderfully written, with scarce source material, like *The Indo-Greeks* by A.K. Narain and *The Greeks in Bactria and India* by W.W. Tarn.

Biography and History

Hayden White had noted that historical narratives follow four basic plots: comedy, tragedy, satire and romance. Quite correctly Dalrymple writes (p. 13): "It is through the human stories of the successes, struggles, grief, anguish and despair of these individuals that we can best bridge the great chasm of time and understanding separating it from the remarkably different world of mid-nineteenth century India." The reference is to the Mutiny Papers which contain facts about the lives of the different individuals living in that time; therefore, each indicated source is a biographical note of a certain common person, contributing to or being affected by, the event of the Uprising. The use of this archived biographical material is laudable and enriching too.

Biography and History are close to each other, as they belong to the same genre, though varying in subjectivity/objectivity. Biography refers to a person's life, where the focus is on the individual and covers in its ambit the other influences, including persons and events, upon the shaping of his life and career. There is necessarily an excess amount of subjectivity, not tolerated in History. Nevertheless, it is an authentic material, though requiring examination in terms of the 'individual:: society' impact, *i.e.*, the degree of impact that a private life makes/receives from the public affairs, at any given time of history.

Quite related to the issue are two instances related to individualistic writings in 1857. One is shared by Amritlal Nagar in *Aankhon dekha Ghadar*, where two Brahmins from Maharashtra travel to Kashi to attend a religious celebration and pass through the cities under turbulence of the Uprising. They wrote their journey accounts from their experience. The other one is the version of Durgadas, a Bengali clerk, stationed at Bareilly, whose perception about the Uprising was noted down in his diary, and used by S.N. Sen in his book *Eighteen Fifty-Seven*, published in 1957. The two writings were more of the biographical kind since the writers were writing their experiences, not at the behest of anyone, but privately for their own personal remembrance.

Dalrymple says further: "Cumulatively the stories that the collection contains allow the Uprising to be seen not in terms of nationalism, imperialism, orientalism or other such abstractions, but instead as a human event of extraordinary, tragic and often capricious outcomes, and allow us to resurrect the ordinary individuals whose fate it was to be accidentally caught up in one of the great upheavals of history. Public, political and natural tragedies after all, consist of a multitude of private, domestic and individual tragedies."

The sum-total of the opinions of people living at a particular time and place certainly has the significance of a 'general opinion'; but the sum-total of biographical accounts cannot become a 'history' of a society for a particular period of time. Often, rather always, large groups of people are "accidentally caught up" in one or the other upheavals of history or Nature, without their own doing, e.g. at Hiroshima and Nagasaki bombings, the Holocaust, the epidemic at Athens, the volcanic devastation by Mt. Vesuvius, and in the present case at the Uprising of 1857. They are victims of the tragedies and their grievances, reactions and opinions are shaped with the affects of their sufferings. Nevertheless, to see the bigger episode "not in terms of nationalism, imperialism, orientalism or other such abstractions, but instead as a human event," amounts to see these sufferers as devoid of nationalistic, patriotic or other feelings and concepts. This mistake is caused by magnifying the microscopic expression of their opinions as found in their day-to-day notes, and imposing it upon the greater event faced by the society or the nation.

Let us take a look at stories that relate human sentiments during important events. It reminds me of an old movie, *Darar* by Baldev Khosa, where the war between two nations breaks a loving family. But it is not true the other way round: nations do not break even if every family breaks, nor do the nations do not unite, even if all of their families unite. The chess-players in *Shatranj ke Khilari*, are nobles, who disliked the British and their designs but do not resist or arise against the forces, because of their indifference to participate as leaders in the situation and reconcile in self-pity. They were not devoid of feelings or loyalty. They, who are sensitive for Kings and Queens of the Chess-board, and actually fight to save their existence; ironically, these players, do nothing in action for their living Nawab of Oudh. Thus, the majority of people are left outside the decision-making, particularly the political moves. Society is not in favour of wars that are often fought on the whims and reasoning of the government in consultation with political or military superiors. Public perception and public decisions are often different than those in actual seat of power, but the intensity of their feelings cannot be measured until consulted.

Conclusion

Briefly, forming opinions on the basis of one's attitude,

approach, knowledge, conscience and the perception of things could be everyone's right; but to pass an effective judgement is the privilege and prerogative of a specialist who practises prescribed methods to evaluate sources, different view-points, and also possesses an unbiased, judicious mind; and acts dispassionately. 'Retelling history' is different from 'reconstructing history', and more complicated than it looks.

BIBLIOGRAPHY

1. Dalrymple, William, *The Last Mughal: The Fall of a Dynasty, Delhi, 1857* (Penguin, 2006).
2. Guillaume, O., "Naïve Anthropology in the Reconstruction of Indo-Greek History" in *The Indian Economic and Social History Review* (*IESHR*), No. 27, 4, 1990, Sage, New Delhi, pp. 476-477.
3. Hibbert, Chrisopher, *The Great Mutiny* (London 1978).
4. Nagar, Amritlal, *Aankhon dekha Ghadar* (in Hindi).
5. Narain, A.K., *The Indo-Greeks* (OUP, 1960).
6. Peter Burke, "History of Events and the Revival of Narratives".
7. Sen, S.N., *Eighteen Fifty-Seven* (Publications Division, New Delhi, 1957).
8. Stokes, Eric, *The Peasant and the Raj* (Cambridge 1978).
9. Stone, Lawrence, *The Revival of Narrative* (1979).
10. Tarn, W.W., *The Greeks in Bactria and India* (OUP, 1954).
11. Yadav, Bhupendra, *Framing History—Context and Perspective* (Publications Division, New Delhi, 2012).

12

Slave-Trade in India (Upto 12th Century AD)

O.P. Srivastava

Although references to slavery are found in the *Rgveda*[1], the earliest references to the slave trade occur in the *Jatakas*.[2] The period between C. 4th century BC and C. 2nd century AD is known for its brisk trade from a number of sources both, indigenous and foreign. Strabo[3] says that the king was waited upon by women purchased from their parents. He also says that by 150 BC, slave trading became a profitable vocation in the East. That an active sea-borne trade was established with India by Egyptian and Greek merchants was testified by the accounts of Eudoxos,[4] Periplus,[5] and Athenaus.[6] Yet a direct references to slave-trade was made by the author of the *Periplus of the Erythrean Sea.* He mentions that beautiful girls for royal harems, as also slaves, were imported to Barygaza. He also mentions the export of women slaves from India to Socotra.[7] Thus at least in the time of the author one of the important articles of the sea-borne trade was human cargo.[8] In the *Justinian Law Digest*, Indian eunuchs have been mentioned as one of the trade commodities subjected to duty at Alexandria.[9] Some black male slaves were also imported to India in the 5th and C. 6th AD from Borneo and other islands of Southeast Asia.[10] The decline of the Roman Empire and the Persian rivalry with the Byzantine Empire rendered the volume of Indian trade, including slave trade, apparently less in the Gupta times than in the first century AD[11], when Pliny had complained of the heavy drainage of Roman money for Indian merchandise of luxury.[12] Slave-trade with the Western world appears to have suffered decline in its volume in this period which lasted till its revival with the contacts of the Arab and Turks. The statement of the Chinese writer Janyun-Hua that human beings are not sold in five Indies and that there are no female slaves[13] does not appear to be correct because there are many pieces of evidence to show that the slave trade existed in early medieval India. In spite of this fact, on the whole slavery was on the decline.[14] The classification of slaves as mentioned in Narada[15] has been generally accepted by the commentators[16] of the early medieval period. Purchased-slave (krita-dasa) was one of the varieties of the fifteen categories of slaves which find mention not only in Hindu[17] but in Jain works[18] also.

Among the literary works throwing light on the slave trade mention may be made of the following: the *Nisithacurni,* the *Samaraiccakaha*, the *Kathakosa*; the *Samaraiccakaha Ganitasarasangraha*; the *Kathasaritsagara* the *Jnatridharmakatha*, the *Uttaraddhyayanatika*, the *Rajatarngini*, the *Lilavati*, *Lekhapaddhati* and the *Prabandhacintamani*. The Muslim and the Arab accounts, such as the *Futuhu-L Buldan*, the *Tarikhu-S-Subuktigin*, the *Tarikh-Yamini*, the *Jami U-L Hikayata*, and *Tarikh-i-Firoz Shahi*, also give information about the problem in question. Though not many, some Indian inscriptions of the early medieval period found in the 3rd, 5th and 8th volumes of the *Epigraphia Carnatica* contain materials relating to the slave trade. A few other inscriptions also throw light on the internal slave trade of this period. With the contacts of the Arabs and the Turks the slave trade, along with trade in general, witnessed a vigorous increase. With the rise of the feudal complex in Indian society,[19] trade and traffic (illegal trade) in slaves got an added impetus from the prevailing internal conditions too. The period also witnessed frequent wars and raids which were the most important sources of slavery from the earliest times.[20] The wars waged by the Arab and Turk invaders led to the capture of numerous prisoners who were often reduced to slavery.[21] This brought about a considerable increase in slave traffic not only in India and other Muslim lands but Christian Europe as well in the early medieval period.[22] We find the testimony of AI'Utbi that after Mahmud's victory over Nidar Bhim slaves were so plentiful that they became very cheap in the same region.

The two documents of the *Lekhanaddhati*[23] state that the girls captured in raids on other kingdoms by indigenous feudal chiefs and soldiers were also sold as slaves. According to Kalhana, King Vajraditya, who ruled from 762 AD is said to have sold many men to the *Mlechchhas*[24] who seem to have been the Arabs of Sindh. Sometimes robbers sold their captives as slaves. The forest tribes are often described as indulging in such activities.[25] *The Upamitibhavapraponcakatha* refers to robbers feeding a man so that he might be sold for a handsome price.[26] *The Kathakosa* relates how Mitrananda fell into the hands of robbers who sold him to some merchants who took him to Persia.[27] It would appear from this that there was a regular export of slaves to Persia. The *Kathasaritsagara*[28] also contains a similar story. The luxurious life of the ruling aristocracy is attested to by the testimonies of art[29] and literature.[30] Temple building, enriched with erotic scenes in this period was mainly commissioned by the kings and the feudal chiefs[31], in which the reflection of their outlook and taste got crystallized.[32] The secular literature of the period also reflects a luxurious court culture.[33] This must have resulted in the increased volume of slave trade and traffic. For the purpose of comparison, it may be noted here that the slaves served a demand of luxury for the rich and the prosperous princes, ecclestical institutions and dignitaries and feudal chieftains even in medieval Europe.[34]

Biological slaves belonged to the male or the female or the third category of eunuchs.[35] We find several references to trade in the first category of the slaves in indigenous literature. The *Kuvalayamala*,[36] the *Kathakosa*,[37] the *Katha-saritsagara*[38] and some Muslim accounts[39] mention trade of male slaves, while the *Ganitasarasangraba*,[40] the *Upamiti-bhavaprapancakatha*,[41] the *Lilavati*,[42] the *Lekhapaddhati*[43] and some Muslim accounts mention trade of female slaves. The *Upamitibhavaprapancakatha*[44] states that eunuchs were sold for lucrative prices. The import of the eunuchs for royal harems is known from Muslim accounts.[45] Though slaves could be technically asked to do any kind of work,[46] in earlier times the majority of them were mainly connected either with productive works or with domestic services in the early medieval period. We find the greater evidence of the sale and purchase of slaves, especially female slaves, meant for domestic services. Thus the slaves were generally purchased for domestic use in this period, but in an emergency they were also used for economic purposes, such as cultivation, etc. In the documents of the *Lekhapaddhati*[47], we find that the duties of the purchased slave girls included outside works, such as cultivation, fieldwork, thrashing, bringing grass, etc. along with other domestic work.

The duties of the purchased slave girls as enumerated in the forms of documents contained in the *Lekhapaddhati*[48] include the following: cutting of (vegetables), pulverizing (spices), smearing the floor (with cow dung), sweeping, bringing water and fuel, throwing away human excreta of her master's family, milking the cow, buffalo, goat, churning curd, bringing grass for fodder, weeding and cutting grass, and other household works (*Grhakarma*), Earlier rules as laid down in the *Arthasastra*[49] show that causing a slave girl to remove dead bodies, urine, the remains of food, hurting or abusing her, or asking her to attend on the master while he was bathing naked, involved the forfeiture of the price paid for her.[50] The use of slave girls as concubines had been prevalent since very early times.[51] In our period this practice appears to have become quite common. Medhatithi[52] made provision for the sustenance of slave girls who were kept for pleasure. The high prices for young girls in the *Genitasarasangraha*[53] indicate that they were slave girls bought for luxury purposes. From the evidence of the *Lekhapaddhati*[54] we can infer that apart from household purpose slave girls could also be used for pleasure.[55] In the first two documents, we find references to slave girls of white complexion, sixteen years old and with pleasing and auspicious limbs.[56] In another document the slave girl is described as having black eyes, a sharp nose, long hair, with all her limbs in proper form. Obviously slave girls were purchased for sexual pleasure as well.[57]

We also find references to slave eunuchs, who were kept in the harem service, especially by Muslim rulers. They were usually bought in childhood and castrated.[58] It appears that eunuchs and castrated boys were used as private attendants upon royal women. Minstrels were also made available for company.[59] Handsome lads were sold in the markets of Delhi during the time of Alauddin Khalji. It is likely that they were used as catamites. We do not find any clear reference to purchase and sale of the boys for sexual pleasure.[60] Inter-regional slave trade continued in our period. This is obvious from literary and archaeological evidence. There is mention of male slaves being taken to *Mahilarajya*, the kingdom of women (probably Kerala in South India[61]), where they were exchanged for gold.[62] This account seems to be exaggerated. However, it may be inferred that male slaves were exported from North to South India for attractive prices. The *Lekhapaddhati*[63] throws light on the capture of a girl from Maharashtra and her sale in Gujarat or Rajasthan. Muhammad Ashraf is of the opinion that the slave eunuchs were imported from Bengal and sometimes also from the farthest Malaya island in the 13th century.[64] This tradition appears to be old. Sometimes the slaves were imported from among the hill tribes who were especially valued because of their strong physique and their power of endurance.[65] The slave as a commodity of trade is also referred to in certain Indian inscriptions. A record[66] dated in the Kali year 4431, falling in the reign of the Hoyasala king Viraballala mentions the tax of 2 Kesu for one slave. Some (at least four) other inscriptions[67] of South India specify slaves as articles on which a toll was charged.

In one of the documents of the *Lekhapaddati*[68], we find references to slave girls offered for sale at Catusapatha L. Gopal[69] is of the opinion that the Catusapatha served as a regular place for the sale of slaves. The choice of the place was with a view to making the sale known to everybody in the city. Certain South Indian inscriptions[70] reveal that slaves were sold in the market along with other articles. Barni[71] mentions the regular sale of male and female slaves in the markets of Delhi during the time of Alauddin Khalji. However, the Catusapatha may have ordinarily served as the regular place for the sale of slaves from the earliest[72] time to this period.[73] In spite of what has been written on slave trade by scholars, the topic of valuation of them on the basis of their different uses has hardly engaged their attention.

More often than not luxury purposes had put the highest premium on the price of a beautiful female slave. Factors like age, sex and other personal qualities of the person offered for sale could also affect the price level. The *Genitasarasangraha*,[74] which throws light on the conditions of the region of South India mentions that a ten-year-old girl fetched 33.33 gold coins while a sixteen-year-old woman could be bought for 20.83 gold coins. A ten-year-old girl could be used for a longer duration for sexual enjoyment than a sixteen-year-old woman. A woman of a light complexion, sixteen years old, with pleasing and auspicious limbs and for multipurpose use, had a higher price, i.e. 504 *Visalpri drammas*.[75] The price of a slave woman mentioned in the second document of the *Lekhapaddhati*[76] is 60 *drammas*. In the above documents of the *Lekhapaddhati*[77] we find two different prices, i.e. 504 *Visalapriya drammas* and 60 *drammas*, for the woman of the same complexion and age, who was meant for the same purposes. Such a difference between the prices of the former and the latter is understandable. It seems that the price mentioned in respect of the former is in silver coins, whereas that of the latter in golden coins but not in gold coins.

The price of a sixteen-year-old woman, in the same region, was less in the time of Mhaviracharya, the author of the *Ganitasarasangraha*,[78] than in the time of Bhaskaracharya, the author of the *Lilavati*.[79] The scarcity of coins in circulation must have resulted in the increased purchasing value of money. Apart from this, the slaves, too, appear to be less in demand in the 9th than in the 12th century. In the later times the demand for female slaves may have increased on account of the growing luxury of the ruling aristocracy. The *Lilavati*[80] dealing mainly with Karnataka, informs us that the price of a sixteen-year-old woman was 32 gold *Niskas* or 32x16=512 sliver *drammas*, while the *Lekhapaddhati*[81] which deals with the region of Gujarat and Rajasthan, mentions 504 *Visalpriya drammas,* or 60 *drammas* (60x8=480) *drammas* as the price of a woman of the same age. It seems that prices for women in two different regions did not vary much. In the Muslim society also beautiful female slaves fetched higher prices, i.e. 20 to 40 *tankas* than did the ordinary female slaves who were sold for 5 to 12 *tankas*.[82] Al'utbi[83] states that in first quarter of the 10th century Mahmud took away prisoners of war in thousands to Ghazna and sold them for 2 to 10 *dirhams.* It appears from this that prices for slaves varied according to their qualities and uses.[84]

The legal procedure for the sale of slaves has been mentioned is some forms of documents in the *Lekhapaddhati*.[85] They provide for the specification of the day, *tithi* and year when the sale of a slave was effected. The names of the buyers, the sellers and the persons who were offered for sale with identifying marks, were also mentioned in one of the documents. The *Panchamukhanagara* was also, sometimes, duly informed. The duties of the slave girls in the buyer's house were set forth in detail.[86] In return, the purchaser was to provide her food, clothes, etc; according to his capacity and the prevailing customs. The punishment which was to be meted out to the slave for the violation of duties was also proclaimed in public. It was laid down that if she committed theft or misbehaved in any other manner in her master's house, or she was interrupted in her duty by virtue of the wealth of her father, brother or husband, while she worked in her owner's house, or committed any dereliction of duty or disobeyed her master, the latter was at liberty to tie, molest or beat her cruelly. If, on being tortured, she ever committed suicide, the master would not incur any guilt or sin. In the *Likhanavali,*[87] we find some model of traditional documents for the sale of male and female slaves. They mention the day, date, and year of the sale and also the village, pargana, district and the state where the sale was made. They also give the word *'amuka'* to indicate the names of those concerned with the sale deeds of slaves, including witnesses and writers. A slave was sold for the price demanded by the sellers or that fixed by the *pancha*. The duties[88] of the slaves are also defined in the documents. These documents do not mention any punishment for dereliction of duty on the part of slaves. It seems that the condition of the slaves in the region of Mithila in the 14th century was somewhat better than in Gujarat, Rajasthan and the adjoining regions.

That slaves were exported to Arabia, Iraq and Persia is evident from indigenous literature and Muslim accounts. The *Upamitibhavaprapancakatha*[89] which throws light on the conditions of Rajasthan and the adjoining regions, mentions that female slaves and eunuchs were sent to the adjoining countries (probably foreign countries also) for lucrative prices. From the stories of the *Kathakosa*[90] and the *Kathasaritasagara*[91] we come to know that the Indian slaves were sometimes, taken to Persia and Arabia. The *Lekhapaddhati* refers to female slaves being shipped overseas and sold in exchange for other commodities. Muslim historian Mir Ma'sum says that the Khalif Abdul Malik, the Sultan of Iran, Iraq and Makran, sent some people to buy female slaves and other specialities of Hindustan.[92] Slaves were not only exported to foreign countries but also imported from Turkistan, Khurasan and China by the Turk rulers of Hindustan. References to import female slaves to India occur in some Jain works,[93] which informs us that female slaves described as Bakusira (from Bakusadesa), Isanika (from the east, probably China), Dhorukini (Tharukini, probably from Arabia), Murundi and Parsi (Persian) were present at the court of a legendary Indian prince, clad in the garments of their own countries. Sometimes, eunuchs were also imported from Malaya Islands.[94]

The attitude of early Dharmasastrakaras that the first two varnas should not trade in human beings, even in the time of distress, continued throughout the early medieval period. It was also laid down in these *Smrtis* that a Brahamana or Kshatriya who indulged in slave trading automatically became a *Vaisya* in seven days. However, we find deviation in actual practice, and kings and feudal lords indulged in slave trading in the early medieval period.

REFERENCES

1. R.V. V, 36; VI, 22, 10; X, 34, 4.
2. *Jatakas,* I, 224, 299, VI, 285, 546; etc. Tr. Fausboll, London, 1962.
3. *Geographia,* XIV, 5-2; vide *Mob Voilence in the Late Roman Republic,* Heaton, p. 12.
4. Ibid., II, 5-12, as quoted by Chakroborty, H., *Trade and Commerce of Ancient India* (c. 200 B.C. c. 650 A.D.), Calcutta, 1966, p. 258.
5. *Periplus of the Erythrean Sea,* ed. Schoff., H.W., New Delhi, 1974, pp. 34, 36, 48.
6. Athenaus Diepnosophisto IV, 4, 6 and V, 2, 39; Cf. Rawlinson, *Intercourse Between India and the Western World,* Cambridge, 1969, p. 93.
7. Periplus, Nos. 31, 34, 35, 36, 49.
8. Mukherjee, S., *Some Aspects of Social Life in Ancient India,* Allahabad, 1976, p. 175; See the article of the same author *Indian Studies, Past and Present,* Vol. VIII, No. 2, 1967; *Slave Trade in Ancient India,* p. 212; See also Rawlinson *Intercourse Between India and the Western World,* p. 47.
9. *Digest of Roman Laws,* XXXIX, XV, 5, 7; vide *Trade and Commerce of Ancient India,* p. 213, fn. 9.
10. Majumdar, R.C., *Suvarnadvipa,* Vol. II, Calcutta, 1938, p. 34, 37.
11. Maity S.K., *The Economic Life of Northern India in the Gupta Period,* Varanasi, 1970, p. 181.
12. *Hist. Nature,* VI. 23, as cited by Aiyangar, K.V.R., *Aspects of Ancient Indian Economic Thought,* Varanasi, 1965, p. 87, fn. 1.

13. Jan Yun-Hua, *"Hui chao's Record on Kashmir", Kashmir Research Biannual,* No. 2 (1962), pp. 119-20; vide, Sharma, R.S., *Indian Feudalism, C. 300-1200,* Calcutta, 1965, p. 59.
14. Ibid., p. 60; See also Yadava, B.N.S., *Society and Culture in Northern India in the Twelfth Century,* Allahabad, 1973, pp. 72-73.
15. V. 27-28, ed. Jolly.
16. *Mitaksara,* II, 182; *Apararka on Yajn,* II-182; *Parasaramadhava,* vyavaharakanda, pp. 239-40.
17. Ibid. *Lakshmidhar, Krtyakalpataru,* vyavaharakanda, 61, p. 371 Sridhara, *Smrtyarthasara,* Poona, 1912, p. 139.
18. Jindasa, *Nisithacurni* II, vide, *Jain Agama Sahitya Men Bhartiya Samaja;* Varanasi, 1965, p. 157.
19. See, Sharma, R.S., *Indian Feudalism.*
20. *Mbh.* IV, 33. 59-60; III, 256, Poona, 1933; *Jatakas* III, 147; IV, 220; V. 497; VI, 220; Trans. Cowell, Calcutta, 1913.
21. Elliot and Dowson, *The History of India,* Vol. II, Allahabad, 1969, pp. 26, 50, 58, 230, 231 etc.
22. *The New Encylopaedia Britannica,* Vol. 16, London 1973-74, p. 858; Cf. Pirence, H., *Economic and Social History of Medieval Europe,* London, 1972, pp. 31, 145-46, 158; Postan, M.M., *Medieval Trade and Finance,* Cambridge, 1973, pp. 132-33.
23. *Lekhapaddhati,* ed., Dalal, C.D. and Shrigondekar and G.K., Baroda, 1925, pp. 41-45.
24. *Rajatarangini,* ed. Visva Bandhu, Hoshiarpur, 1965, IV, 397.
25. Suri, H., *Samaraiccakaha,* II, p. 91 f., ed. Modi, M.C., Ahmedabad, 1935.
26. Siddharsi, *The Upamitibhavaprapncakatha,* ed., Peterson, B., Calcutta, 1899, pp. 404-405.
27. Trns., Tawney, C.H., *The Kathakosa,* New Delhi, 1975.
28. Somadeva, *Katha-Sarit-Sagar,* Tr. Tawney (The Ocean of Stories) London, VII, 3, 3-51.
29. Vidya Prakash, *Khajuraho,* Bombay, 1976; Agrawal, V., *Khajuraho Sculptures and Their Significance,* Delhi, 1964; Gangoly, O.C., *Konarka,* Calcutta, 1955; Mitra, D., *Konarka,* New Delhi, 1976; Barnett, L.D., *The Proceedings of Indian History Congress,* 1941, pp. 261 ff. etc.
30. *Dosarupuka* of Dhananjaya; *Naisadhyacarita of* Sri Harsa etc.
31. Yadava, B.N.S., *Society and Culture in Northern India in Twelfth*

Century, p. 327; Desai, D., *Erotic Sculpture of Northern India. A Socio-Cultural Study*, New Delhi, 1974, p. 39.

32. Desai, Loc., cit., pp. 39-40.
33. Yadava, op. cit., p. 329.
34. Postan, M.M., *Medieval Trade and Finance*, Cambridge, 1973, p. 306.
35. *Mitaksara*, III, 36, *Manusyapadeaavisesat-stripunnapunsakaha Grahanam)*; The *Upanitibhavabhavaprapancakatha*. p. 404 f.
36. *Suri*, U. *Kuvalayamalakaha*, p. 46.
37. Ibid., p. 157.
38. Ibid., VII, 3. 3-51.
39. Elliot and Dowson, pp. 50, 124, 161-62, 298-99.
40. Ibid., p. 89.
41. Ibid., p. 404 f. as quoted by Sharma, *Chauhana Smrata Prithaviraja Tritiva Aur Unka Yuga*, p. 74.
42. Ibid., p. 102.
43. Ibid., pp. 44-45 op. cit., p. 74.
44. Ibid., op. cit., p. 74.
45. Elliot and Dowson, p. 118, Vol. III, p. 118, Vol. III, p. 196; Ashraf, op. cit., p. 188.
46. Medbatithi on Manu, VIII 415.
47. L.P. pp. 44-45; as quoted by A.K. Majumdar in his *Chalukyas of the Gujarat*, Bombay, 1956, pp. 345-49.
48. Ibid., Cf. *Treisastisalakapurasacarita*, Vol. III, Baroda, 1949, p. 248.
49. *Arthasastra*, III, 13.
50. In the *Likhanavali* of Vidyapati (14th c. AD) there are two model of traditional documents for the sale of male Sudra slaves, who had to perform, in addition to the work of tilling, palanquin bearing bringing water and carrying luggage for their master *rautas* and *Thakkuras*, pp. 42-44.
51. *Arth*. III, 13, Katyan, 728; *Jatakas* I, 225, 451 f; III, 409 444; VI, 110, 117, 285; Yaju mentions *avaruddha* and *Bhujisya* female slaves for sexual enjoyment.
52. On Manu, IX, 143.
53. Ibid., p. 89.
54. Ibid., pp. 44-45.
55. L. Gopal also infers this that slave girls were of ten kept rather for sexual pleasure than for their utility as maids. *Economic Life*

of Northern India, p. 80.

56. Ibid., op. cit., pp. 44-45, 47.
57. In the Likhnavali, we find a model of document for the sale of the slave girl for marrying. Cf. Herodotus, that the virgins were in Taxila for marrying, op. cit., pp. 83-84.
58. Ashraf, op cit. p. 188.
59. Elliot and Dowson, Vol. II, pp. 161-62.
60. Manu (XI, 174, IX 67), Yajn. (III, 234, 242), Visnu (XXXVIII, 5; LIII, 4) and Smrityarthasara (p. 139) say that the act of sexual enjoyment with boys caused the sin leading to loss of caste.
61. Agrawal, V.S., *A Cultural Note Kuvalayamalakatha,* in the *Kuvalayamalakatha,* ed. Muni, J.V., (S.J.G.) Bombay, 1970, p. 119.
62. Suri, U., *Kuvalayamalakatha,* p. 46, vide Motichandra, *Sarthavaha,* Patna, 1966, p. 199.
63. Bhaskaracharya, *Lilavati,* with Hindi Trns, Jha, L. Varanasi, 1976, p. 45.
64. Ashraf, K.M., *Life and Conditions of the People of Hindustan* (*1200-1500*), Published in J.A.S.B. (Letters), Vol. I, 1935, p. 188.
65. Ashraf, *Life and Conditions of the Hindustan,* p. 188.
66. No. 70 K of Kolar; vide Iyer, S. Subramania, *Ancient Dekhan,* Fernhill, 1917, p. 44.
67. *Epigraphiacarnatica* VIII, Sorab 237; E.P. Car., V. Belur 75; E.P. Cat. III, Malavalli 95; Nellore Inscriptions, III, on gole 132, 213 of 1918.
68. E.P. Car, V. Arsikere, 22-1188 AD; 157-1154 AD as quoted by Appadorai in his book, *Economic Conditions in Southern India* (*1000-1500*), Madras, 1936, Vol. I, p. 44.
69. *The Economic Life of Northern India,* p. 74.
70. *Epigraphia Carnatica* V. Arsikere 22 (1188 AD) 157 (1154 AD); E.P. Car, VIII, Sorab 237; E.P. Car; V. Belur 75; E.P. Car, III, Malavallai 95; *Nellore Inscriptions,* III, on gole 132; etc. No. 70, K. of Kolar, Vide op. cit.
71. Elliot and Dowson, Vol. III, p. 196.
72. Herodotus mention that the virgins were made to stand at the crossing of four roads for sale in Taxila. *Persian Wars,* I, BK. I, Ch. 196, pp. 83-84, as quoted by Soletore, R.N., *Early Indian Economic History,* Bombay, 1973, p. 406.
73. LP., p. 44.
74. P. 89, The author of the *Ganitasarasamgrah* enjoyed the

patronage of Nrpatunga or Amoghavarsh (815-877 A.D.) of the Rashtrakuta dynasty which extended from Manyaketa to far northwards.

75. LP. p. 44.
76. Ibid., p. 45.
77. Ibid., pp. 44-45.
78. Ibid., p. 89.
79. Ibid., p. 102.
80. Ibid.
81. Ibid., pp. 44-45.
82. Elliot and Dowson, Vol. III, p. 196.
83. Ibid., Vol. II, p. 50.
84. Barni writes that the price of an young domestic slave was fixed from 17 to 18 *tankas,* while the handsome lads could be bought for 20 to 30 *tankas* in the markets of Delhi during the time of Alauddin Khalji (1296-1316 AD), op. cit., p. 196.
85. Ibid., pp. 45-45.
86. Supra.
87. Ibid., pp. 42-44.
88. Supra.
89. Sharma, D., op. cit., p. 74.
90. Ibid., p. 157.
91. Ibid., VII, 3, 3-51.
92. Elliot and Dowson, Vol. I, p. 118 fn. 2. Biladuri, however, gives a different account that the king of the Isle of Rubies (Ceylon) sent as present to Hajjaj (705 AD), 'the government of Iraq and Makran certain Muhammadan girls, who had been born in his country the orphan daughters of the merchants who died there, but the ship in which the girls were embarked was attacked and taken away some barks (pirates) belonging to Meds of Delhi', Ibid., Vol. I, p. 118.
93. *Nisitha Sutra,* IX, 28; *Uttaradhyayantika,*VI, p. 39; *Jnatridharmakatha* I. p. 21, vide; Jain, H.L. *Jain Agama Sahitya Men Bhartiya Samaja,* pp. 161, 256.
94. Ibid.

13

Under the Theme of Rock Art:
Signature of Ancestors–Its Meaning and Classification

A.K. Dubey and Sachin Kumar Tiwary

ABSTRACT

The authors in this paper present a systematically prepared chart on Rock Art, for the first time. The methodology which we use here is to categorize the rock art sites on the basis of its physical location such as 'Above the Water and Under the Water' and further divides the former into two categories namely, 'Above the Ground and Under the Ground'. Within these divisions, the authors methodically list the various types of Rock Art available such as the Pictograph, Petroglyph, Geoglyph or Petro-forms, Pictograph-cum-Petroglyph. Also the present paper aims at introducing a new term in the field of Rock Art studies. It is well known that the term Rock Art is used to denote the artistic expression using the bare rock as the medium. These have been grouped under two main categories, namely pre-historic and historic on the basis of the material used, style, etc., and they were available in various forms such as paintings, etchings, engravings, impressions, etc. So far all the rock art irrespective of their location have been grouped under one category alone. The present author basing his study on the various research materials of different scholars came across an entirely new concept, namely 'Under Water Rock Art'.

Keynote: Under Water Rock Art, Relief Art, Pictographs, Petroglyphs, Geoglyphs, Pictographs- cum-Pictographs.

Introduction

Art is the manifestation of innate beliefs, outlook and purpose expressing the materialized vitality of activity of man born out of his experience. (Mitra, 1927: 211). Art in any form is an expression of the inner self of an individual, person or group of people. The questions raised are those concerning the various purposes art serves within the context of pre-literate societies and the nature and function of symbolism. The evidence of first petroglyphs was reported from Almora in Uttaranchal in India by Henwood, 1856:204-05 as early as 1856. The first discovery of prehistoric rock paintings was made in India in 1867-68, 12 years before the sensational discovery of Altamira in Spain by Archibald Carlleyle (Smith 1906: 185-195) at Sohagighat, Kaimur region in Mirzapur district of Uttar Pradesh.

Origin: Primitive people may have got this idea from observation of the sinuous arrangements of sand on river valley by water waves or in deserts by wind or footmarks of animals on river beds. Or drawings might have originated accidentally when a man scribbled playful or natural markings on rock walls suggesting an animal to which he added more lines of his own to increase its resemblance. Even objects of nature might have inspired them for practising art activities.

Purpose of Rock Art: Archaeologists believe that the types of stone chosen and their position in the landscape can provide clues to the role of rock art in the prehistoric world. Many theories have been put forward to account for rock art but no one has yet been able to unlock their secrets. It is very difficult to say, if we could in imagination enter the mind of ancient artists as they set to work would probably find thoughts like these:

1. Defining Territory: Rock art is often found on, or close to, striking natural features such as 'monumental' outcrops, unusual boulder formations, plunging waterfalls, caves, rivers and cliffs. These dramatic locations evoke emotional and imaginative responses and may have formed an important part of the mythical landscape of the past. Connections to specific places can also be created through shared social events, natural catastrophes, or more personal experiences.

2. Route-Markers: In some areas the deliberate positioning of carvings on relatively high ground, often with extensive views, and along possible 'route-ways', seems to point to a connection with movement across the land. Decorated stones are often found overlooking natural harbours, at the entrances to possible routes inland, close to mountain passes, and along the edges of valleys, associations with specific routes are problematic since few actual prehistoric tracks have been identified. Further, an understanding of both route-ways and the extent of views requires a more detailed understanding of the nature of prehistoric vegetation than is currently available. "I have had a strange dream, may be it is important; a picture will help me recall it".

3. Sacred Spaces: Rock art is often found in locations which may suggest a strong 'spiritual' element to the role of the carvings. In hunter-gatherer communities, 'luminal' locations, where dark meets light, where mountains touch the sky, or the sea reaches the shore, are often considered the domain of supernatural beings or ancestors. The occurrence of carvings in these places suggests a religious significance to the motifs, perhaps used to mark the focus of links between past and present, the living and the dead, or between real and spiritual worlds. The presence of rock art within ceremonial and burial monuments also suggests connections with ritual activity, although these associations tend to occur later in the Neolithic and into the Bronze Age and may reflect a change in the significance of rock art.

4. Natural Influences: One recent strand of research which could provide new insights into the way carvings were originally perceived has studied how the motifs relate to the shape and fabric of the rock on which they are carved. Observations suggest the motif-makers looked closely at the rock surface to see what motifs would fit onto it, taking into account features such as cracks, indentations and other irregularities. Indeed, relationships have been identified between the size and nature of the motifs, and the size and shape of 'frames' formed by natural fissures on the rock surface. It has been suggested that natural features, such as hollows and cracks, may have been regarded as ancestral images to be incorporated, mimicked, or even erased by the application of new motifs, with both natural and artificial markings attracting the addition of new images. Natural features on the rock and their relationship to the motifs may form an important part of our understanding of the carvings themselves.

5. Public versus Private: The public nature of rock art in the landscape suggests that it was intended for a wide audience, although carvings may have been viewed by different groups of people at different times. Complex panels, often found at the outer edges of the settled landscape, may have been visited only occasionally during hunting expeditions or seasonal grazing. The groups using these panels would therefore have needed precise information. By contrast, simple carvings in the lower, settled areas would have served a more stable population who shared the same body of knowledge. But simple relationships between 'style' and social structure do not always hold and it is also argued that the simpler the art, the greater the range of meanings that can potentially be drawn from it.

6. This is our territory, I will post this notice to keep others out.

7. I have done a mighty deed, I want everyone to know about it.

8. I must pay homage to my gods, I will create their image and ceremonies.

9. My clan and kin are the greatest—we claim this area as ours.

10. This animal is important to me, I think about it a lot, I will draw its likeness.

11. I am bored, I will draw something to pass the time.

12. I have returned from a long journey, I will try to show my path way across the Land.

13. My friend and I have had a great ceremony, I will record it.

14. My chief has asked me to go here and put up some signs along the trail. I will get it over with as soon as possible.

15. Some declare land.

16. Some record ceremonies in the life of an individual or community.

17. Some give instructions which still work today on where and how to hunt game.

18. I have a new artistic design in my mind; I will record it before I forget.

Drawing on Stone: Every culture on earth produces visual art which is an expression of its creative self. The evolution of shared symbolic systems is argued representing the development of a human cognitive capacity. For many indigenous cultures around the world, the only surviving record of their earliest artistic endeavours is rock art. (McDonald, ed. 2006: 96)

"Rock art as the term implies is the art on rock, any type of artistic activities found on rock is rock art (Mathapal, 1995:1) which types of art, it is still in debate. Is it right that a prehistoric stone tool, which was made by our ancestors should be classified under rock art? I agree because it had been done on the stone which is a small part of rock. Ajanta, Ellora, Elephanta, etc. any art item that has been done on rock, that is under rock art, because here again it has been done on rock. Like inscriptions which had been done in those times on rock itself or part of boulders or a smallest part of rock that could be a stone slab, that is also rock art. Why because engraving which is under rock art study but why not inscriptions (only those which have been done on rock). But all works of art on rock are not rock art."

However it is applied to all types of artistic expression noticed on the natural rock surface of caves[1], shelters[2], (plain surface of ceiling and walls), outcrops (plain or undulated surface) and boulders. They are efforts at communication and are truthful messages in the sense that all signatures or symbols serve to convey mental messages on stone. It is also known as "rock picture" (Clegg, 1985: 35-47), its antiquity ranging from the prehistoric to the historical period continues without any obstacle.

Rock art is broadly found in three types:

(a) **Petroglyphs** or the **extractive art** (designs, carved, abraded or otherwise cut into cliffs, boulders, bedrock, or any natural rock surface, like: Relief art[3], Engravings[4], Hammering, Chiselling, Abrading, Incising[5], Pecking[6], Battering[7], Gouging[8], Scratching, Cup-marking[9], Bruising, Dotting and Etching) (McDonald, ed., 2006: 60).

(b) **Pictographs** or the **pigment art** (Rock paintings-designs painted in similar locations). It does not include geoglyphs, or petroforms-designs formed by rock alignment on the ground. (Polly S., et al., 1985: 237) Technically, pictographs may be further divided into four groups; transparent colour, opaque colour, dry colour and stenciled pictographs. Pictographs are also known as "rock paintings".

(c) **Geoglyphs** or **intaglios** are made by placing rocks on the ground to form an image or by clearing the ground of rocks to outline an image. It is massive designs made on the ground and are best seen from the air. The ground is cleared of rocks to make huge figures or shapes. These are not as common worldwide, they occur in the southwest of the US in California and Arizona, or in South America. According to another definition that "a large motif (usually > 4m.) or design produced on the ground, either by arranging clasts (positive geoglyph, stone arrangement/alignment, petroforms, earth mound) or by removing patinated clasts to expose unpatented ground (negative geoglyphs).

(d) **Pictographs-cum-Pictographs** means all those forms of rock art, in which after petroglyphs, pictographs have been done, in the removed rock surface. Like this art we have seen in Orissan rock art and Hazaribagh region of rock art.

Such a categorization of rock art becomes necessary to have a micro-analytical study of the art and may help in its interpretation and solving conservation problems as well.

Chart for Rock Art Classification

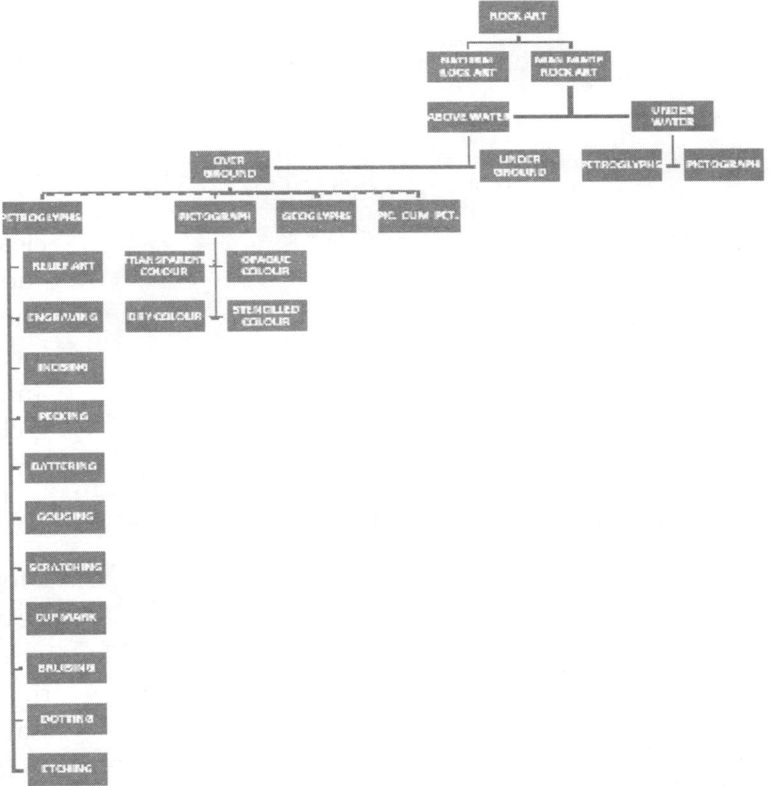

Under Water Rock Art: The term 'Under Water Rock Art' can be explained in a similar way as 'Marine Archaeology'. It refers to those rock art sites which had existed on the coastal plains or on the fringes of water bodies which in due course of time got submerged into the water due to various reasons, the cause of which may be natural such as changes in the earth's crust and the subsequent rise of the water level or even man-made causes such as modern developmental projects. So this specialized field of Rock Art Studies deal with those paintings which already got submerged or on the verge of submersion and analyses its various problems such as the causes of its submersion (if natural), it's preservation and conservation problems, methods adopted for its exploration and documentation, etc. Such kind of evidences are noticed from France Islands (Northumberland), Cosquer cave (France), Island of Melanesia (Australia), Island of Lifou (New Caledonia). So far no such term has been used anywhere to describe any rock art site.

Conclusion

Rock art represents an irreplaceable cultural heritage, and the state is not necessarily its most ardent protector. Independent, preferably international peer review is essential. Perhaps it could be argued that international rock art scholars should not concern themselves with what happens to Portuguese rock art. The rock art is not the property of any state or private individual. It is the property of all of humanity past, present and future. It is to be treated as such, and not as a hostage of an inexperienced, secretive and deceptive technocracy. The entire art site is a sacred monument. As a fact of history, it is inseparable from the human race. In this context rock art reflects the relationship between people and the land. The pre-historic rock paintings consist of the Mesolithic and Chalcolithic cultural traits. Most of the Mesolithic paintings are an expression of the relationship between human beings and animal life. The depiction of paintings shows lifestyle of hunting and gathering society particularly by the Microlithic using people. This idea was already known to the Mesolithic society and that is why the community express in themselves rock art. The Mesolithic people have tried to explain the life activity of their society. They have given bigger expression about their challenge of life through rock art paintings. The execution of painting works by Mesolithic painters is sometimes in very inconvenient places like high rock walls or ceilings which could only have been done by using elaborate ladders and scaffolding. The Chalcolithic paintings are sometimes executed in superimposition overlapping the early paintings. These paintings also consist of the same aspects like expressions of their lives. Thus the first step is the proper identification and safeguarding the rock art which remains located in the little known areas and to record their names on a map with others. For the purpose of future referencing, it is absolutely essential to compile a detailed and illustrated inventory of rock art in accordance with the location and state of the preservation of the sites in a state or region. Such a work should include all the known sites and particulars of their art and archaeological contents. Drawings of the paintings should be prepared. In India there are already legislations for the protection of cultural heritage sites but they need some change or modifications and implemented strictly. Bodies like the Archaeological Survey of India (ASI) and Department of Anthropology, Government of India, should serve as the nodal agencies in such a project. Universities and State Department of Archaeology, Rock Art Society of India, IGNCA, IFRAO and other qualified institutions could be assigned a specific area comprising rock art sites to collect and document in instalments. The work can be undertaken as a project under the University Grants Commission (UGC) or the Indian Council of Historical Research (ICHR). If possible, UNESCO could be approached for the purpose. After all, this work is a conservation point, it is essential to know that all application in this work should be reversible. It is time to realize and meet our responsibility for preservation and further study of rock art as being an important part of our proud cultural heritage. We should at least endeavour to make and have records of this art and culture for the edification and knowledge of the future generation.

NOTE

1. **Cave** is a geological formation consisting of an underground enclosure with access from the surface of the ground or from the sea.
2. A **rock shelter** is a shallow cave-like opening at the base of a bluff or cliff. Another term is rock house.
3. **Relief** in sculpture, three-dimensional projection from a flat background. In alto-relievo, or high relief, the protrusion is great; basso-relievo, or bas-relief, protrudes only slightly,
4. **Engravings** are pictures, patterns, or designs cut into rock faces by pecking, scraping or grinding with a tool.
5. **Incised** in archaeology and the plastic arts refers to cutting into the surface of a medium, for example stone or wood. It often refers to the use of a "V"-shaped tool to carve out the design. Writing carved into stone tablets or columns is often referred to as "incised".
6. To make (a hole) by striking repeatedly with the beak or a pointed instrument.
7. A uniformly steep slope in a retaining wall or pier; inclination is expressed as 1 foot horizontally per vertical unit (in feet).
8. A scooped out or deeply carved indentation in soft rock, made with a gouging tool.
9. **Cup-and-ring** art is ore reverent, being found across northern Britain. It uses mostly curvilinear motifs, including simple ups, grooves, rings, and variations of these. These carvings are found in a much greater variety of locations, including on outcrops, boulders, cliffs and rock shelters, but are also associated with airns, stone circles, and standing stones. Most are found on horizontal or gently sloping surfaces, and natural features such as fissures may be incorporated into the design. They are fluid' in their design and they tend to be found in open, 'public' positions.

REFERENCES

Clegg, J., 1885, Comment on D. Groenfeldt's "The Interpretation of Prehistoric Art" in *Rock Art Research*, Volume 2 (I), pp. 89-90.

Henwood, W.J., 1856, "Megalithic Culture at Devidhoora in Almora", *Edinburgh New Philosophical Journal* (New Series), Edinburgh, pp. 204-05.

Mathapal, Y., 1975, Rock Paintings of India, An Orthographical Interpretation, *Bulletin of Deccan College*, Research Institute, Poona, Vol. 35-73, Nos. 3-4, pp. 83-93.

Mitra, Panchanan, 1927, *Prehistoric India: It's Place in the World Culture*, University of Calcutta, Calcutta, p. 211.

McDonald, Jo, 2006, *Archaeology in Practice*, ed. Jane Balme and Alister Paterson, Blackwell Publilishing, pp. 59-96.

Mucklroy, K. 1978, *Maritime Archaeology*, Cambridge University Press, New York, p. 34.

Polly, Schaafsma, 1985, *Form, Content and Function: Theory and Method in North American.*

Pradhan, Sadasiba, 2001, *Rock Art in Orissa*, Aryan Books International, New Delhi, pp. 3-4.

Schiffer, Michael B. (ed.), "Rock Art Studies" in *Advanced Archaeological Method and Theory*, Vol. 8, p. 237.

Smith, V., 1905, "Pigmy Flints", *The Indian Antiquary*, Vol. 6, pp. 185-195.

14

Hierarchical Society and Social Justice (6th Century BC)

Jhinkoo Yadav

The Vedic theory of social organization was essentially propounded to make the society progressive in all walks of life. Every skilful class according to one's own merit was authorized to shoulder the responsibility of one's own class. Early Rgvedic society was like a human body of which different limbs represented the different social classes, based on division of labour and duties assigned to them. We find a simple faith and devotion in early Vedic society for a better and happier life. But, in later ages, our society became the victim of orthodox feelings by proclaiming the superiority of upper varnas which germinated a sense of inequality and hatred in the Vedic social order.

In the 6th century BC, Lord Buddha and Lord Mahavir launched the social reforms movements by preaching the Sramana religion against orthodox feelings, inequality and hatred in society. The Sramana is derived from 'Sam'which means equality, fraternity and love. Gautam Buddha states in *Digh Nikaya* that a Sraman is one who has got rid of *bhavanas* (feelings), viz. friendliness, compassion, sympathetic attitude and equanimity.[1] He further states at another place that a real Sramana is one who has aquired perfectly a purified conduct, speech, thought and mode of living by controlling the sense organs, moderation in eating, being intent on vigilance, being possessed of mindfulness and clear consciousness, remote longing, to get rid of doubt and getting rid of five senses, etc.[2] According to Lord Buddha, man himself is responsible for his own deeds. Sramanas always discounted the rituals and established a path of moral, mental and spiritual development as the only means of escaping from the miseries of the world (*sansar*) which was an obstacle in the way of salvation. Some Western scholars like Winternitz, Rhys Davids, Leuman and others have opined that the origin of the Sramana cult is in protest against the orthodox Vedic cult.[3] Prof. S.B. Deo has also stressed the point that Sramana did reveal the anti-Brahmanical feelings as they were not satisfied with the degenerated Brahmana priesthood.[4] Some scholars observe that early Buddhism represented a reaction to certain aspects of Vedic religion.[5] In others' opinion it appears to be a new synthesis of the non-Aryan tradition of yatis or munis as Sramanas from the early Vedic age.[6] But certain facts cannot be denied that Buddha was a 'social reformer' in as much as he condemned the caste system, preached the equality of men and perceived the connection between the economic welfare and moral development of the individual.[7] In B.R. Ambedkar's opinion, Buddha stood for equality, viz, no caste, no inequality, no superiority, no inferiority, etc.[8] These evidences prove that Lord Buddha launched a social reform movement against the orthodox feelings of the Vedic social order and preached the lessons of equality, fraternity and love amongst the people to equalize the society in regard to social, religious, economic and education etc. This was the instance of first movement of Social Justice in Indian History. Lord Buddha's mission was to equalise all sections of Indian people through his preachings during the 6th century BC. This treatment of equality in respect of better opportunities and status to all is truely a treatment of human with a human beings. He preached the lesson of equality and totally ignored the Brahmanical social order which was based on *varna,* caste and the clan system. He admitted the Sudras and other lower class people to his religious order (Dhamma Sangh) along with Brahmanas, Kshatriyas, Vaisyas and other higher caste people. Lord Buddha also protected the interest of the Sudras and other lower class people by encouraging them to have a better place in the society equal to those of the Brahmanas. This was the sense of social awareness among the poor and depressed class people. Through his religious movement he encouraged them to move ahead of the orthodox Brahmanical social order. Buddha proclaimed that skilfulness and good deeds were the main criteria for high positions in the society not *varna,* caste, clan or class.

In the light of social justice moved by Lord Buddha against the social evils, Walter Rubens states that the Sudra remained a member of the lowest rank, even if he was rich.[9] He further states that ideologists of despotism laid stress on the hereditary principles connecting exploitation with birth in every rank and contrasting as much as possible the Aryan with non-Aryans.[10] He further states that probably in no other society is there a rank like that of the Brahmanas somehow similar to Levites or ancient Jews, nor do we have a counterpart of the Indian Sudras in any society except the few helots of ancient Sparta and some other Dorian states. This statement of Walter Rubens indicates that Aryans were conquerors over non-Aryans. The conquerors ruled over non-Aryans and treated them as slaves. They suppressed them and enriched their own economy and social status on their labour. For this sake they (Aryans) appropriated the products of village communities to themselves leaving as little as possible to non-Aryans. This became the main cause of conflict in ancient Indian society. It was further framed in a law to regulate the division of products. There was a question of who would till the fields, to breed the cattle and to work in handicrafts and what part of the products would be given to the various social classes. According to Rubens, the need of Dharm was stressed in Dharmasutra to avoid the conflicts.[11] So, the sword of Dharma was used to establish their superiority in all respects. Hence, our ancient Indian social order was manipulated by the upper varnas in the name of religion for better facilities.

In spite of the above arguments stated by Rubens, Rhys Davids observes that there was no hard and fast line determined by birth regarding the social order.[12] The Buddhist text *Jataka*[13] refers to a Kshatriya who successfully works as a potter, basket maker, reed worker, garland maker and cook. It is further stated that a Sethi also works as a tailor and as a potter who still retained the respects of his high born relations.[14] But evidences of these social equalities were the result of Lord Buddha's movement towards social justice. As evident, is seen that the beginning of the 6th century BC saw the downfall of the Mauryan empire, a large number of Sudras and the weaker sections of Indian society were not entitled to get their right dues and privileges like the Brahmanas and Kshatriyas. They led a life of agriculturists, labourers and slaves. The Dharmasutras give us extensive information regarding the slaves who were employed for the family work.[15] Slaves were also being employed for agricultural products in the Mauryan period.[16] This fact is also revealed from the literary sources that Brahmanas were not treated as outcastes nor were they the victims of sins or punishment at the cost of adopting different lower caste occupations, i.e. shopping; meat selling, animal husbandries and artists, etc.[17] Like other weaker castes, they were not compelled to follow their own Varna Dharma and kings and monarchs could not dare to punish them for violating the Varna Dharma.

The Buddhist text *Vinaya Pitak*[18] states that a man can criticize another man in view of his caste, name, deeds and crafts, etc. Here, we find the two categories, i.e. Vena, Nishada, Rathakar and Lukkas were put in the category of lower castes and Brahmanas and Kshatriyas were put in the category of higher castes. Higher caste people were treated as a privileged class, hence, they led a very luxurious life along with high positions, whereas lower class people led a very hard life. The Apastamb Dharmasutra[19] states that people born in lower varnas may get birth in higher varnas in the next birth by following the systems of Svadharma. The term Svadharma means to perform the duty of one's own varna or caste. Manu also gives a ruling that people will get salvation by following Svadharma (Varma Dharma) properly, but those who do not follow the principles of Varna Dharma will suffer a lot.[20] Dharmasastrakaras have also given directives to the kings and monarchs to compel the people to follow their Varna Dharma. The Apastamba Dharmasutra[21] states that the kings had enough power to give orders for the punishment to their subjects who violated the principles of Svadharma. Gautam Dharmasutra[22] also gives the same ruling. These are the religious rules to employ the weaker sections of ancient Indian society in their services for the betterment of the privileged class. It is evidently seen that from the beginning of the 6th century BC a certain sections of the lower class lived on the different occupations and crafts, such as hunting, following fishery, weaving, smithy, pottery, etc. These artisans and craftsmen supplied their skilled labour for the production of particular economic requirements of social consumption. Besides these, the fifteen disapproved occupations *(Karmadan)* as referred to in the Bhagavati sutra[23], involved both physical and mental labour without which they could not be carried on for a day. These are hunting of deer *(Migavittiya)*, fishery *(Matsyapalan)*, charcoal maker *(Ingala Kamma)*, cutting and selling of forest woods *(Vana Kamma)*, selling of carts *(Sadi Kamma)*, transport business *(Bhadi Kamma)*, cultivation *(Fodi Karmma)*, ivory business *(Dant Vanijia)*, lac business *(Lakkha vanijia)*, wine business *(Rasa vanijia)*, poison business *(Visa vannijia)*, act of crushing sugarcane, etc. with machine *(Jantpilana Kamma)*, castration of bulls *(Nillachana Kamma)*, act of draining or drying up the big tanks, lakes, etc. *(Saradah Talayapari-sosanaya)* and act of running brothels *(Asaipsanaya)*. In Buddhist literature, we find bird catchers, cart-makers, aboriginal tribesmen, mat-makers, barbers, potters, weavers and leather workers.[24]

The references to these artisans and other professional men give an idea of various arts and crafts taken up by certain sections of people as an occupation to earn their livelihood, such as—weaving, dying and cleaning, mining and metallurgy, blacksmithy, ivory, fuel industry, leather works, perfumery and toiletry etc.[25] These occupations gave birth to several castes in ancient India to earn their livelihood which put a stamp of social hierarchy. Later on the social recognition was given to the person born in his own clan and these clans gave birth to the caste system which took the shape of higher and lower status.

Hence, Lord Buddha denounced this caste system, challenged the Brahmanical superiority, questioned its Brahmanical religious sanction behind it and all in all it was not permitted within his religious order of monks *(Dharmma Sangha)*. Though he did not uproot the caste hierarchical social order because of its productivity but he launched a movement to uproot the evil notions of high and low, superiority and inferiority, hatred, orthodox feelings, enmity, etc. and paved the way for equality, fraternity and love among all for the sake of social justice. Buddha's religion was based on an individual's religion, through which he wanted to uproot the social evils by establishing a sense of equality, truthfulness, fraternity and love amongst everyone by breaking the boundaries of high and low, rich and poor, caste, class, region and religion. He emphasized *pudgala* for this social equality. He says that *pudgala* is the main cause of social ills, i.e. sufferings, impermanence and nothingness and can be modified only when many individuals improve their nature by tending to move towards the dilution of their individuality.[26]

REFERENCES

1. *Digha Nikaya,* 1/170.
2. Ibid. 1/170; *Majjhima Nikaya,* 1.271.
3. Jain, Bhagachandra, *Jainism in Buddhist Literature,* p. 3.
4. Deo, S.B., *History of Jain Monachism.,* p. 56.
5. *Encyclopedia Britannica,* Vol. III, p. 403.
6. Pande, G.C., *Studies in the Origins of Buddhism,* p. 326ff.
7. Om Prakash, *Conceptualization and History in Early Indian Socio-Economic Studies,* Allahabad, 1992, p. 105.
8. Ambedkar, B.R., *Buddha and His Dhamma,* Bombay, 1957, pp. 301-306.
9. Walter Pubens, 'Outline of the Structure of Ancient Indian Society', p. 88, in *Indian Society: Historical Probings,* New Delhi, 1974.
10. Ibid., p. 88.
11. Ibid.
12. Rhys Davis, *Buddhist India,* p. 40.
13. *Jataka,* V, 290.
14. *Jataka,* VI, 372.

15. Sharma, R.S., *Sudron ka Prachin Itihas,* p. 147.
16. *Arthasastra,* 2/14.
17. *Manu,* 11/11/1-71.
18. *Vinaya Pitaka,* IV, p. 6.
19. *Apastamba Dharmasutra,* 2/11/10; 2.2.3.
20. *Manusmriti,* 10, 130.
21. *Apastamba Dharmasutra,* 2, 10, 12-16; 2, 11, 1-4; 2, 27, 18.
22. *Gautama Dharmasutra,* 11, 30.
23. *Bhagavati Sutra,* 1, 8, 65; 7, 6, 288; 8, 3, 330.
24. Rhys Davis, op. cit., p. 40.
25. See Sikdar, J.C., *Studies in Bhagvati Sutra,* p. 294.
26. Udna, 86-87, quoted by Om Prakash, op. cit., pp. 108-109.

15

Socio-Cultural Ethos of Buddhism

V.K. Pandey

The religion of Buddha is distinct not only because of its new doctrinaire basis but also due to strong socio-economic concepts that the founder of the religion propounded in order to give vent to a new kind of social concerns are sometimes so strong and entirely different from the pre-existing notions that he has often been termed as 'revolutionary'. There is no doubt that he gave a reformative touch to several ideas and practices that were infringing upon the basic tenets of humanity and were restraining the full-flow of human potential.

The religious movements are not simply the pathways to the realization of spirituality but are very often interlinked to the socio-cultural ethos of the contemporary times. A case in point is Buddhism which came into existence during the 6th century BC—a century widely regarded as 'an age of far-reaching religious reforming activity not only in India but over the whole of the Ancient World.'[1] Gautama Buddha, the founder of this religious movement, was possessed with the superb ingeniousness and practical vision to assimilate the new emerging ideas into his system and give a new interpretation to almost all the basics concepts which had crept into the social fabric of his times making it stagnant and rigid.

The materialistic historiographers such as Gordon Childe attribute them to a change in social being, while idealist historiographers locate them in the progress of thought through its autonomous dialectics.[2] however, for us, no single reason can be assigned for these changes, as they were the products of several composite factors.

There is no denying the fact that important changes did take place in society in India during the age of Buddha and the centuries preceding and succeeding it. Before the advent of Buddhism, we meet in the Brahman texts of the later Vedic times a society which still to a considerable extent is tribal in character, ruled by kings who, though wealthy and powerful, have only a rudimentary governmental machinery in the form of *ratnins*. According to R.S. Sharma "certain material conditions favoured the rise of Mahajanapadas in the 6th century BC. The use of iron for crafts and agriculture was an essential features." Likewise, the beginning of large-scale settlements in the alluvial soil was also one of the characteristics of the 6th century BC.

The early Buddhist period was a period of expanding material culture, with far wider trade relations than in the previous period. In the Vedic texts, cities are hardly referred to but now, in the time of Buddha, popular towns and cities exist in all districts of the Ganga valley. A great and apparently very rapid change had taken place in the structure of life and society.[3] New groups of merchants and skilled craftsmen were gaining in wealth and influence.[4]

In later Vedic texts, the *rajanya* , a relative of kinsman of the *raja* played the diminutive role of a chief but, now he practically came to be replaced by the *Kshatriya* order in the Pali texts. The Jain and Buddhist monks, who had no place in the Brahmanical hierarchy lent greater support to the emergent ruling order, for they accorded the *Kattiyas* the first place in social ranking.

The confederation of the Vajjis, the most important of these republics, was still, apparently, a force to be reckoned with, but there is a clear indication that its assembly, the governing body of the confederate tribes, was rapidly becoming inadequate to cope with new situations, and the tribal structure was undergoing great strain. Towards, the end of Buddha's life the Vajjian confederacy was overwhelmed by the rising kingdom of Magadha.[5]

That Buddha had a vision of an ideal society, is clear enough from the organization and functioning of his order. People coming from every walk of life and of all castes and communities mingled in it and pursued their highest spiritual ends without any discrimination. Every member of this order was supposed to be a part of its functioning organized on the principle of equity and functioning on a democratic pattern with all proprietary rights contained in the overall fraternity, the Buddhist monastic order stands as a microcosm of a model society. It would be appropriate here to recall the words of D.P. Chattopadhyaya in *The Lokayata: A Study in Ancient Indian Materialism*, "the Buddha created an illusion of liberty, equality and fraternity by modelling his Sangha on the tribal values. Whereas in reality these values were being trampled upon in the world outside the Sangha".

The reformative vision of Buddha was not confined to the arena of society alone. He had a vision of a new economic order which gradually unfolded itself in the wake of a second urbanization. He is found lending his ideological support to the processes of this new emerging phenomenon directly or indirectly. In several contexts, the terms *gama* (village) and *nagara* (town) have been alluded to as representing two types of cultural complexes. A number of terms related to the former such as *gamadhamma, gamavasinadhamma, gamadaraka,* etc. occurring in the Pali texts refer to a kind of wicked conduct. Here the culture of the villages conveys a kind of rusticity, an unrefinement, whereas that of a town (*nagara*), a refined or civilized one.

Obviously, Buddha had a natural preference for the towns which had all the essential infrastructure to support the huge community of the monks and nuns. It is just not a chance, that most of the Viharas of the Buddhists are found located in the vicinity of the towns. In an analysis of Thera and Therigatha done by B.G. Gokhale, it has been shown that 86 per cent of monks and nuns referred to in them came from the towns such as Sravasti, Rajgriha, Kapilvastu, and Vaishali. In the Nikayas, Buddha is mentioned preaching most of his sermons in the cities of Sravasti, Kaushambi, Vaishali, etc. He also spent most of his *varsavasas* (rainy season) in the cities of Sravasti and Vaishali. In fact cities and towns and the people living in them are found providing basic amenities and material support to the fraternity of the Buddhists, hence, it is quite understandable why Buddha offered his ideological support to the city and city life. He also accepted the other concomitants of urban life, such as wealth generation through the pursuits of *Kasi* (agriculture), *Gorakkha* (animal husbandry) and *Vanijja* (trade and commerce) and by the practice of a number of *sippas* (arts) mentioned in the Pali texts. Wealth was esteemed and its accumulation was regarded as a laudable activity. In the Madhura Sutta of the Majjihima Nikaya, wealth is mentioned as a determinant of social status. It has been shown that even a person of Sudra origin having wealth may obtain the services of a Brahmana. Buddha gave vent to new economic changes characterized by the second urban revolution. It had led to the growth of towns and commerce; the development of trade had resulted in the emergence of a class of fabulously rich merchants; and organization of crafts into guilds had awakened the spirit of enquiry among the people. They turned to finding freedom from the bonds of custom rather than to preserving the traditional way of life.[6]

In the middle of Ganga valley, there was Kutuhala-Salas for relaxation and debate. These were not only shelters for religious teachers during the rainy season for they attracted the audience as well. Urban life released a degree of curiosity and free thinking which was employed by some of the contemporary teachers, as they were anxious to address large audiences.[7] The Kutuhalasalas were maintained by wealthy citizens or through royal patronage and were clearly important locations for debating a variety of doctrines.

Buddha lent his clear-cut support to the new economic atmosphere promoted by agriculture (*kasi*), animal husbandry (*gorakkha*) and merchandise (*vanijja*), referred to several times in the early Buddhist texts. The texts like *Sutta Nipata* underline the significance of intensive agriculture, made possible with the use of iron ploughshares and new farming techniques. Buddhism found its wrong supporters among the big landlords (*gahapatis*) and wealthy merchants (*srethins*) who, unlike the Vedic period. were offered an active participation in the religious life eventually leading to their raised social status as recognition. Merchants and traders are found organizing in guilds, carrying their trade and commerce in groups in a caravan of hundreds of carts and practising both inland and sea-bound trade. Contrary to the injunctions of the Dharmasutras, money lending, earning profits through interests and sea-faring became the order of the day as is obvious from numerous references to these activities in the early Buddhist texts. Thus Buddhism promoted the new urban economy in its gospel.

It is generally believed that the Buddha was a great social reformer, a believer in the equality of all human beings, a democrat and that his efforts for the emancipation of women and lower castes created a sort of social revolution in society.[8] A proof generally advanced in support of the view that the Buddha was a social revolutionary is based on the assumption that he attacked the caste system as it existed at that time. Buddha dealt firmly with the evils which had a sickening effect on the society. Caste was one of them. Buddha inherited a hierarchical-static society water tight compartmentalization. The four Varnas had split into castes and sub-castes of superior (*ukkattha*) and inferior (*nicha*) categories, which were determined on account of their birth in a particular caste. The Brahmanas being at the apex of the caste-pyramid naturally claimed their social superiority based on birth that was demolished by Buddha in a number of *Suttas* and *Nikayas* and in other texts. In the *Sonadanda Sutta*, the Brahman Sonadanda declares that there are five prerequisites for being regarded as Brahman-Varna (pure descent on both sides), *jati mantra* (knowledge of the Vedas), *sila* (virtue) and *panditya* (learning). But when the Buddha presses him to declare what is indispensable out of these five, the Brahmana agrees that only the last two are necessary to make a person Brahman. Obviously *sila* and *panditya* are the traits and not the varna or jati or mantra which characterize a Brahman. In the *Assalayana sutta* when the Brahmana Assalayana claims that Brahmana is a superior varna, the Buddha tells him that people of all the varnas are the same human species, capable of interbreeding. In the *Vasettha Sutta* when the Brahmanas came to him with the problems: does one become a Brahmana by birth or deed, he explains the difference between species (which differ in physical features) and human classes (which depends on the vocations of man). A man may become a trader, a soldier or may adopt any other profession. But a Brahmana who has high moral qualities and is detached and wise, one does not become a Brahmana by birth. Thus Buddha analyzed the notion of superiority of a person, not on the basis of his birth in a particular caste or class but in the matrix of right conduct and deeds. Buddha also struck at the root of ritualism and vehemently denied the efficacy of animal sacrifice in a number of passages occurring in the Pali texts. He declares that senseless killing of animals and sacrifices serves no religious purpose; it is sheer cruelty towards those mute creatures. In the *Samannaphala Sutta*, it has been alluded that a monk should never indulge in the destruction of life; he should rather develop the feelings of friendship and compassion towards all living beings. He advocated the simplicity in religious life, shunned all kinds of externalities and rituals and emphasized that the ultimate end of a religious life should be to create a virtuous, noble and enlightened man. According to Ambedkar, "No caste, no inequality, no superiority", all are equal. That is what Buddha stood for.[9] Rhys Davids has stressed that Buddhism ignores completely and absolutely all advantages and disadvantages arising from birth, occupation of social status and sweeps away all barriers and disabilities arising from the arbitrary rules of mere ceremonials or social impurity.[10] Buddha opposed the caste hierarchy based on birth as was advocated by the Vedic religion. The Buddhist protest against the caste system, whatever its limitations, was not 'revolutionary' in another sense also. It was something new or radical; it was shared by all contemporary religious sects.

It is also certainly true that Buddhism recognized the right of and gave opportunities to even Shudras to enter the Sangha. But what was revolutionary about it? The other contemporary ascetic sects gave the Shudras the same opportunities and rights. Even the Gita accepts it as the right of every body to achieve emancipation. One more notable contribution of Buddha to the contemporary society was opening the space to womenfolk for religious participation. This may again be called distinctive as their right to religious participation was drastically curtailed in the Brahmanical fold. With admission of Mahaprajapati Gautami and her ilk, he opened the door of his order for female members and founded the Bhikhkhuni Sangha with a separate code of discipline. There is no doubt that the code of discipline as perceived for the nuns in the Vinayapitaka places them in a secondary position compared to monks. With a number of restrictions around them they are definitely not at par with their male counterparts. Yet granting them with a right to religious participation may be taken to be a progressive step, given the contemporary stereotypes of a highly patriarchal society. Some historians have made an attempt to differentiate the religious and social aspects of Buddha's attitude to women. It has been urged that though from the standpoint of religion, which demanded high moral discipline on the part of a monk, the Buddha appears to be anti-women but in social aspects, he did not teach difference between men and women.[11]

His system also avoided extreme type of asceticism and therefore could attract the common man who was wary of extreme self-mortification. For a lady devotee the practice of his Dhamma needed very little extra expenses, thus providing a striking contrast to the costliness of the Vedic rituals. His denunciation of slaughter of animals in the name of religion received widespread support and his condemnation of the superiority complex of the Brahmans appealed to the non-Brahmana masses.

Contrary to the ideal 'Trivarga' practised in the Vedic society, Buddha propounded the ideal of 'Chaturvarga' with the concept of 'moksha' as the highest ideal of life. With this notion, Buddhism cut man loose from the sense of dependence on gods and also struck a blow to the doctrines of social obligations. It replaced gods by the force of karman; what man receives he does not owe to God but his past actions. Further, as man cannot avoid the moral consequences of his actions, he must eschew, egoism, violence, etc which are according to the Buddhist view, the main evils in pursuit of morality.

Buddhism brought the process of social change to a climax with an endorsement of a socially articulated individualism that was within a framework of self-control and ethical behaviour. Thus it could promote a rational and open society but one, which nevertheless was, based on monarchy, private property and the patriarchal family. G.B. Upreti rightly observes: Buddhism's "positive, rational and socially-oriented individualism firmly fastened the individual to 'well-earned private property' at the economic level, to a 'caring partriarchal family' at the social level and to an 'orderly-state' at the political level. If the individual moulded his behaviour and thinking at the anvil of non-egitism not only did he himself became a rightful holder of private property, an ideal householder and a good citizen, but also enormously contributed to the formation of a viable economy, a strong and solid social structure and a healthy and durable state."[12]

In the discourse pertaining to a layman's happiness (domestic and otherwise) (*Gahapati Sukha*) foremost is mentioned the satisfaction derived by a layman from the possession of wealth obtained thorough righteous means (*atthi sukha*). However, the Buddha warns the man against the tendency to become a slave to the mere accumulation of wealth for its own sake. It would lead to both physical and mental suffering later. Adequate means of livelihood to support oneself and family, to help relatives and friends, and to distribute among the needy and deserving, would lead to contentment and inner satisfaction. This in turn, would result in the moral and spiritual development of man.

Buddha welcomed the emerging classes of landholders, artisans, merchants and traders and exhorted them to be conscious of their duties. He stood for new initiatives, entrepreneurship and enterprise. He advocated the use of new technologies, promoted trade and commerce and practice of monetary economy, the elements which were largely instrumental for the emerging urbanization and the urbanism of the time.

Buddhism is both a path of emancipation and a way of life. As a way of life it interacts with the economic, political and social belief and the practices of the people. It is felt that the time is now most opportune to make known to the world each of the above aspects of society within the framework of Buddhist ethics and the basic principles of Buddhism. The progress of a country depends ultimately on the progress of the individual.

Thus, the social and cultural concepts of Buddhism were so articulated by its founder that they not only lent voice to the contemporary aspirations, but also stood for a progressive and rational society where one can perform his duties righteously and realize the highest end of his life.

REFERENCES

1. *Cambridge Ancient History*, iii, p. 49.9.
2. Pandey, G.C., *Studies in the Origin of Buddhism*, p. 310f.
3. Basham, A.L., 'The Background to the Rise of Buddhism' in *Studies in History of Buddhism* edited by A.K. Narain, New Delhi 1980.
4. Ibid., p. 16.

5. Sharma, R.S. 'Material Progress, Taxation and State Formation in the Age of Buddha' in *B.P. Sinha Felicitation Volume*, edited by Bhagwant Sahai, New Delhi, 1987.
6. Ibid.
7. Thapar, R., *From Linkages to State* , Bombay, 1984, p. 153.
8. Nehru, Jawaharlal, *Discovery of India,* 1946, p. 141, Rai, M.M., *From Savagery to Civilization*, p. 9, Ambedkar, B.R., *The Buddha and His Dhamma*, pp. 301-6, Pratapchanda, 'Buddhism as Instrument of Social Change', *Studies in Religion and Change*, edited by Madhu Sen, 1983, pp. 81-92, Narau, P. Lakshmi, *The Essence of Buddhism*, 1976, Chapters 4th and 5th; Prasad, N.K. *The Democratic Attitude of Buddha*, 101, 120, 162, pp. 299-310.
9. Ambedkar, B.R., *Studies in Religion and Change*, pp. 101-10.
10. Dialogues, iii, p. 78.
11. Madhu Sen, Ibid., pp. 101-10.
12. Upreti, G.B., *Early Buddhist World Outlook in Historical Perspective*, New Delhi 1997, pp. 143, 168.

Contributors

Zill-Ur-Rahman Khan, Former Professor, Department of Physics, Aligarh Muslim University, Aligarh.

Om Prakash, Former Professor, Department of Ancient History, Culture and Archaeology, University of Allahabad and Vice-Chancellor (Ex.), M.J.P. Rohilkhand University, Bareilly.

H.K. Sharma, Professor and Head, Department of Political Science and Director, Academic Staff College, University of Allahabad, Allahabad.

P.R.R. Nair, Professor and Head, CRCG, Indian Institute of Corporate Affairs, Ministry of Corporate Affairs, Government of India, New Delhi.

U.P. Arora, Former Professor, Greek Chair, School of Language, Literature and Cultural Studies, Jawaharlal Nehru University, New Delhi.

Anup Kumar, Head, P.G. Department of History, Gandhi Faiz-e-Aam College, Shahjahanpur.

R.P. Tripathi, Former Professor, Department of Ancient History, Culture and Archaeology, University of Allahabad, Allahabad.

A.K. Sinha, Professor, Department of Ancient History and Culture, M.J.P. Rohilkhand University, Bareilly.

J.N. Pal, Former Professor, Department of Ancient History, Culture and Archaeology, University of Allahabad, Allahabad.

Abhay Kumar Singh, Professor, Department of Ancient History and Culture, M.J.P. Rohilkhand University, Bareilly.

O.P. Srivastava, Former Professor, Department of Ancient History, Culture and Archaeology, University of Allahabad, Allahabad.

A.K. Dubey, Professor, Department of Ancient Indian History, Archaeology and Culture, Banaras Hindu University, Varanasi.

Sachin Kumar Tiwari, Assistant Archaeologist, Patna Circle, Archaeological Survey of India, Patna.

Jhinkoo Yadav, Director, National Research Institute of Human Culture, Varanasi.

V.K. Pandey, Associate Professor, Department of Ancient History, Culture and Archaeology, S.B. College, Jaunpur.